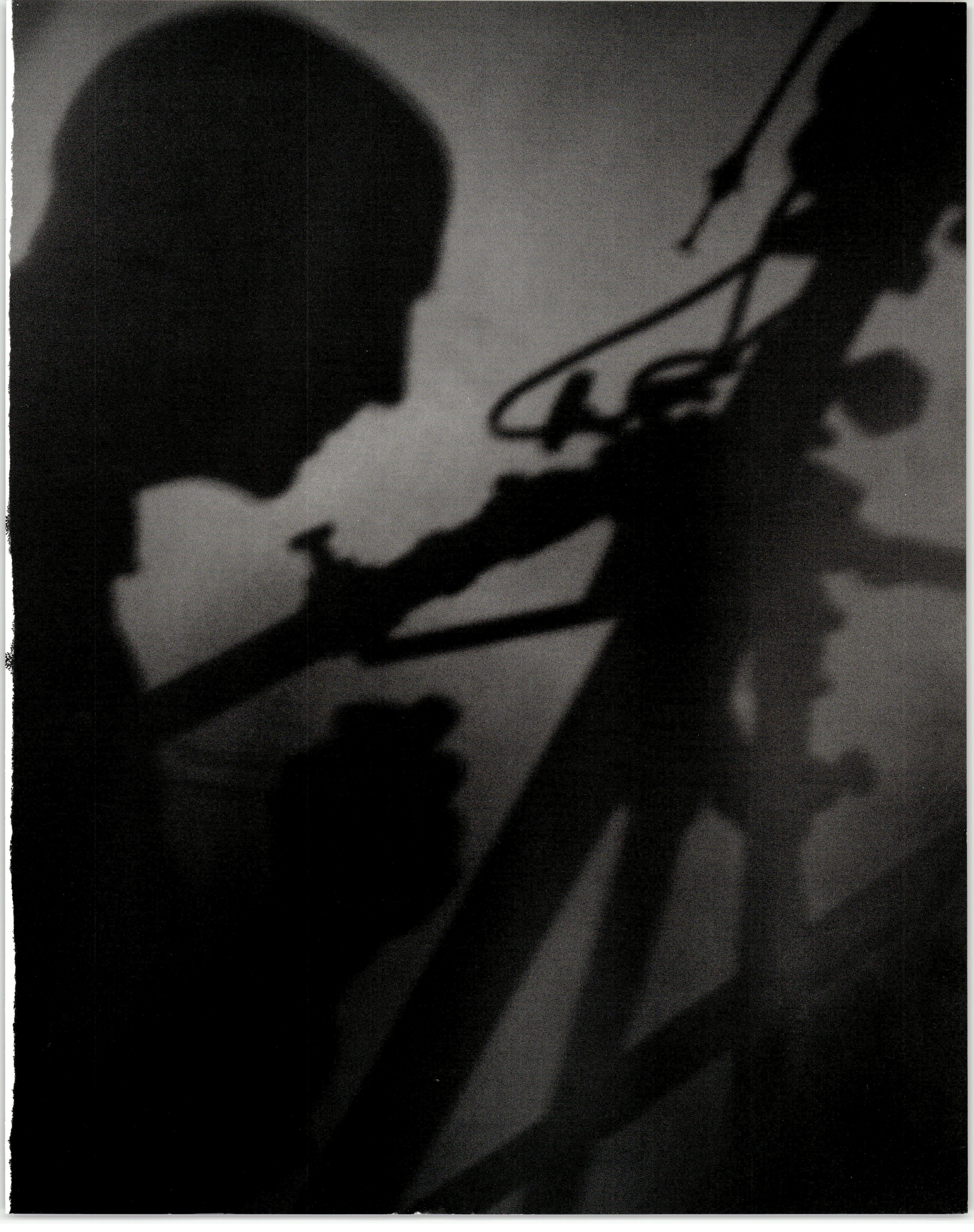

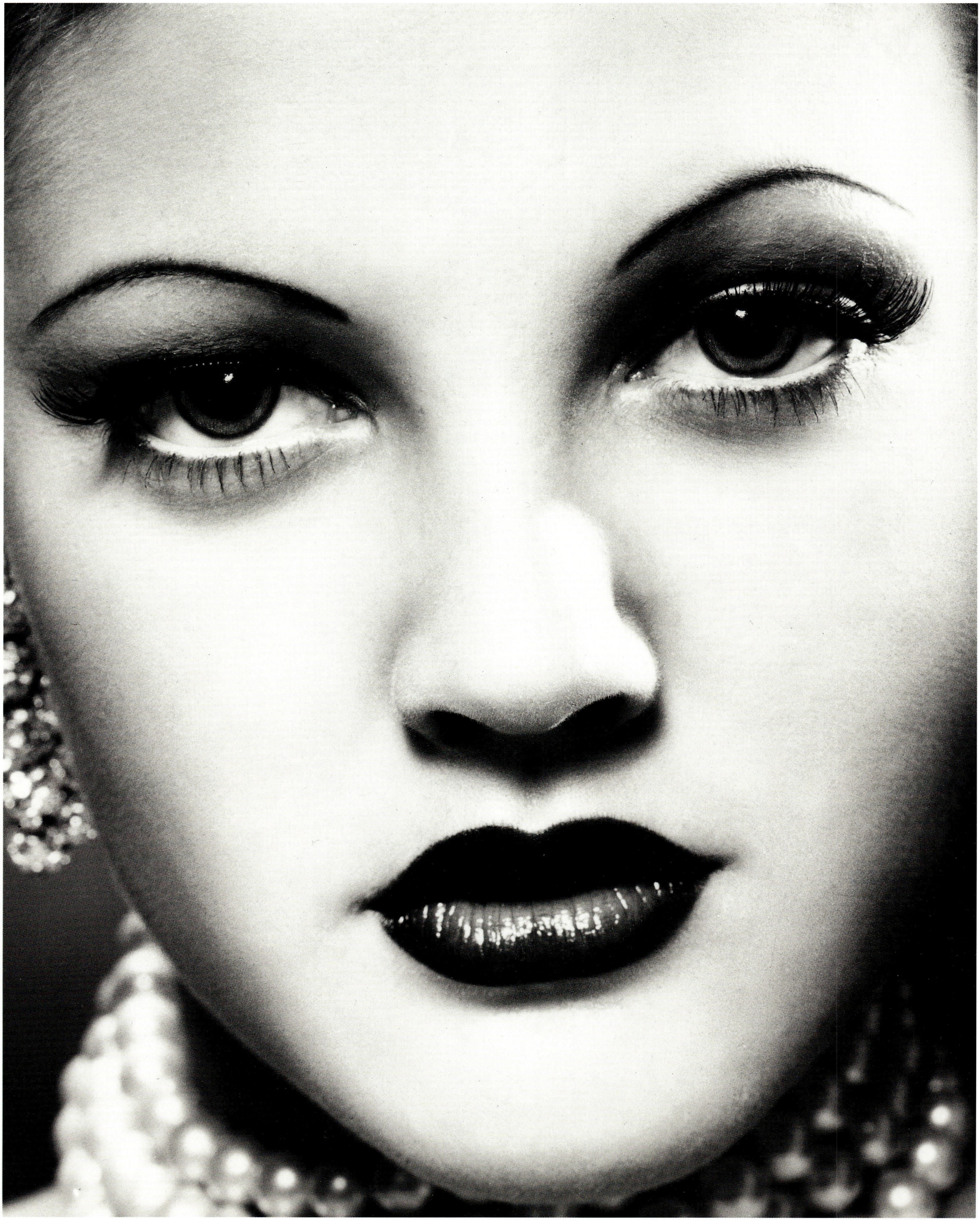

ABOUT GLAMOUR

LEN PRINCE

INTRODUCTION BY DOMINICK DUNNE

SIMON & SCHUSTER EDITIONS

Published by Simon & Schuster

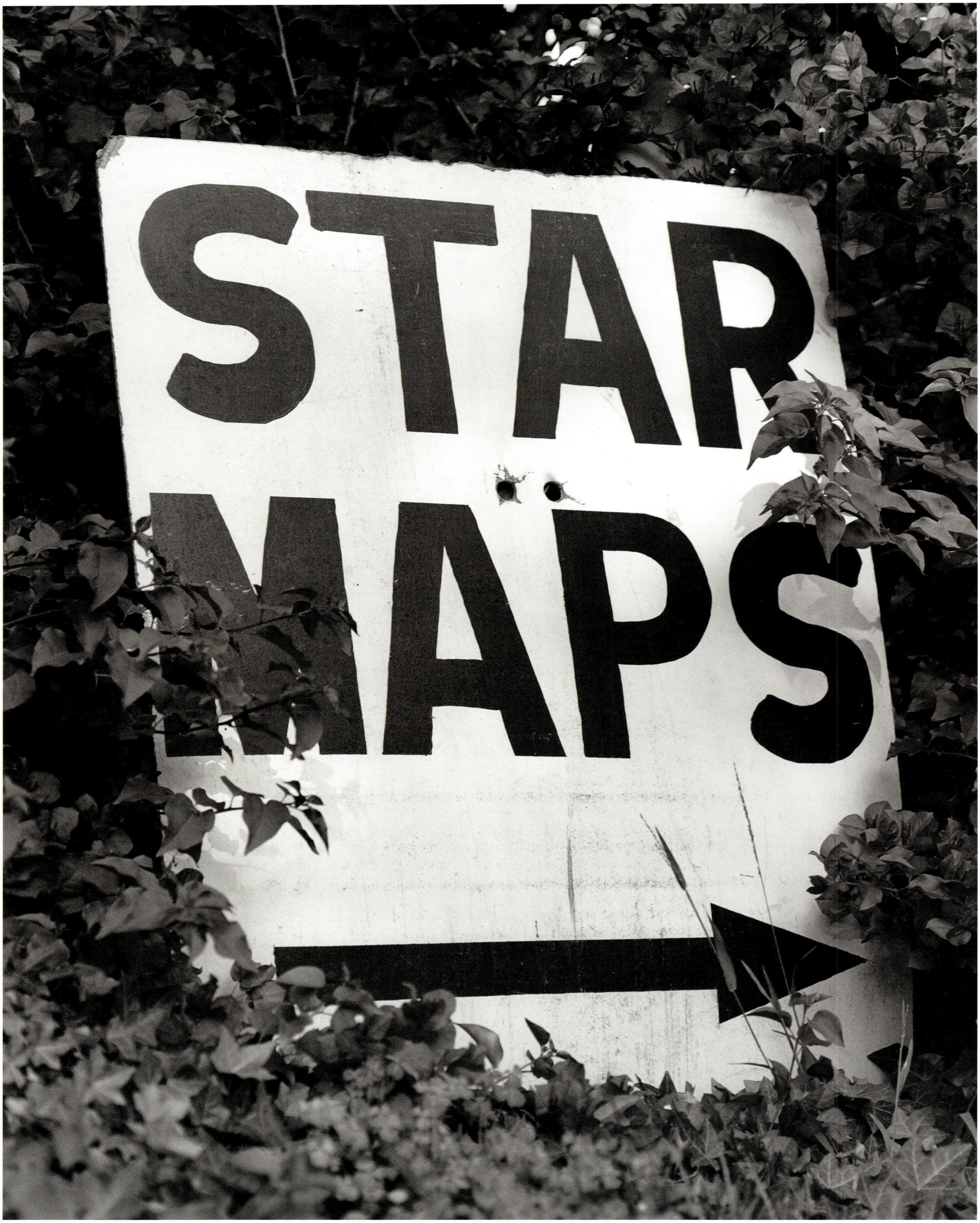
STAR
MAPS

Thinking about writing this introduction to Len Prince's dazzling book of photographs evoking the bona fide glamour of film stars from an earlier Hollywood era, all sorts of memories began to come back to me. Years ago, in my West Hartford, Connecticut, boyhood, long before I knew that one day I would be a part of that extraordinary thing called the film industry, I was mesmerized by Hollywood and those inaccessible beyond-our-reach stars of that period when movie stars were really movie stars. Gary Cooper, Joan Crawford, Tyrone Power, Loretta Young, Greta Garbo, Carole Lombard, Clark Gable. On and on, the whole lexicon of them. I even like the remote ones that no one remembers anymore, like Frieda Inescort and Gale Sondergaard. When my brothers were reading comics, I was reading *Screen Guide*. I kept pictures of Brenda Joyce, Andrea Leeds, and Michèle Morgan. I loved Ann Sheridan and Ida Lupino in *They Drive by Night*. I read every word about Constance Bennett's romance with Gilbert Roland, after she was washed up with the marquis de la Falaise, who used to be married to Gloria Swanson. I cried when Jean Harlow died, and was sure it was the peroxide in her hair that killed her at twenty-six. I knew that the bridesmaids at Deanna Durbin's wedding to Vaughn Paul were dressed as shepherdesses and carried crooks instead of flowers. I saw Bette Davis in *Now, Voyager* seven times, and fifty-five years later, I can still remember her last line: "Don't let's ask for the moon. We have the stars," said Bette to Paul Henreid, as they kissed and smoked cigarettes.

I knew all the movie star scandals. How I heard at age nine or thereabouts that Paulette Goddard had performed fellatio on the director Anatole Litvak under the tablecloth at Ciro's in Hollywood, I haven't any idea, but I believed it with all my heart, and longed to meet Paulette, who'd married Charlie Chaplin, Burgess Meredith, and Erich Maria Remarque. I knew the contents of Paul Bern's suicide note when he shot and killed himself during his honeymoon with Jean Harlow, even though Louis B. Mayer, who founded MGM, and Howard Strickling, the head of publicity at MGM, destroyed it at the scene of the crime before the cops arrived, so there wouldn't be a scandal before Jean's next picture opened. The studios took care of their own in those days. When I saw photographs of Cary Grant and Randolph Scott sharing a house together on the beach in Santa Monica, I thought to myself, "Uh-oh." But then Cary married Barbara Hutton, the five-and-dime heiress, and everything was all right again.

For a couple of decades, in a previous career, I became a part of all that. I arrived in Hollywood in 1957, ready for a career in television and movies. The old studio system that built the stars was coming to an end, but I saw the last of it. I was under contract to 20th Century–Fox. Darryl Zanuck reigned supreme at Fox and was always putting his French girlfriends under contract. When there was a premiere of a Fox film, the young actors and actresses under contract would be teamed up together to attend, and the actresses would be dressed to the nines in gowns, jewels, and furs lent by the studio that afternoon. There was a huge back lot where Century City is today. My office was in a bungalow near Jerry Wald's bungalow. Jerry was the most important producer on the lot. Marilyn Monroe was the queen of the lot, beloved by everyone except the front office. The 20th commissary was the place to be at lunchtime. Cary Grant was making *An Affair to Remember* with Deborah Kerr. Frank Sinatra was making *Can-Can* with Shirley MacLaine.

I have never quite understood the secret of my social success. I was still shy in those days and didn't say much, although I stared a great deal at what I was beginning to see. I was invited to high places long before I had a right to be invited, as far as my accomplishment in the industry was concerned. I have begun to envision myself as a sort of Hollywood *Zelig*, the character created by Woody Allen, always there, always remembering, but unnoticed himself. I saw the very people I used to read about. At a party at the Humphrey Bogarts', I stared at Judy Garland, who was their next-door neighbor, as she stood in the curve of the piano and sang in her heartbreaking style, and watched Spencer Tracy, who wasn't drinking that night, eat an entire box of chocolates as he listened to Judy. One night the famed producer Ray Stark and his wife, Fran, who was the daughter of Fanny Brice, gave a party for Aly Khan before he married Rita Hayworth. I stared at Gary Cooper, in black tie, and Merle Oberon in pale blue satin and wondrous emeralds, as they roared with laughter together at a private joke. When the music started, Norma Shearer, the personification of elegance, never missed a dance with Martin Arrouge, her ski instructor second husband who bore a striking resemblance to her first husband, the brilliant MGM executive Irving Thalberg, who died at thirty-six. Thalberg, who was immortalized in F. Scott Fitzgerald's novel *The Last Tycoon*, masterminded Norma's career and made her one of MGM's greatest stars. Another night, at the producer William Frye's house in the Hollywood Hills, Tyrone Power had

Lana Turner totally mesmerized as he talked to her by the swimming pool overlooking the lights of Los Angeles below. A year later, Lana's lover, the gangster Johnny Stompanato, was knifed to death by Lana's daughter, or so they said, in a house very close to my own in Beverly Hills. At the Gary Coopers', I heard the sublime Audrey Hepburn's surprisingly boisterous laugh as she joked with Billy Wilder. On Sunday morning all the Catholic stars turned up for the ten o'clock Mass at the Good Shepherd Church in Beverly Hills, which people jokingly called Our Lady of the Cadillacs, so well off were its parishioners. Once I saw Clark Gable speed away after Mass with his fifth and final wife, the beautiful Kay Spreckels, in a brown Mercedes Benz convertible, looking exactly how a movie star is supposed to look. Jane Wyman went there, and Cesar Romero, Gary and Rocky Cooper and their daughter Maria always stopped to chat on the sidewalk before heading for their gray Bentley, while Rosalind Russell and Loretta Young blew farewell kisses, and Roz then ran for her black Rolls-Royce. At a private party at Romanoff's one night, Marilyn Monroe, who looked as if she had just been stitched into her very tight green sequined dress by the wardrobe department at Fox, which she probably had been, taught the ladies of Beverly Hills, like Mrs. Billy Wilder and Mrs. Fred de Cordova, how to sashay across a room the way she did, all the time roaring with laughter as the ladies followed in her wake. William Holden danced with Jennifer Jones, and Marlene Dietrich, looking fantastic, smoked cigarettes and remained sullen to Michael Rennie, with whom she was then involved. That night at the party, Gene Tierney was my favorite. Beautiful, dazzling, she sang into the ear of the man she was dancing with. "A trip to the moon on gossamer wings. Just one of those things." Watching all those people interact with one another—everyone famous, or rich, or beautiful, or powerful—I knew I had a ringside seat to watch their magical world.

Those were heady times. But it was changing. Everyone could feel it. Twentieth sold off its back lot. The studios stopped having contract players. Television had arrived in a big way. Norma Shearer told me she would never own a television set, because television had destroyed movies. Style was going out. The great stars were dying off. Clark Gable, Humphrey Bogart, Gary Cooper, Tyrone Power, Cary Grant, Bill Holden. Zelig, again, I had known them all. Merle Oberon's emeralds were auctioned off at Christie's, and Mrs. Aaron Spelling, of the new wave of wives of moguls, bought them with much fanfare. A new type of leading man came in. And a new type of leading woman. Ties came off. Jeans came in. Beards were the rage. And long hair. Different kinds of pictures were being made. I even produced one of them: *The Panic in Needle Park*, about heroin addiction, which was the first starring role in pictures for Al Pacino. The Warners, the Cohns, the Zanucks, the Balabans, the very families who started the studios and loved to make movies, were gone, replaced, and not long remembered. Agents took over the studios.

I'm not knocking the way it became. That's the way of the world. Times change, tastes change. I'm glad I got to see what I saw. I'm a believer in social history, and I wish there had been more records of it. And then a strange thing happened. In 1996, *Vanity Fair* needed a picture of me for its annual movie issue, which comes out every April, and I was sent to Len Prince's studio by the photo department to have my picture taken in the style of a reporter in an old black-and-white movie. In Len's studio on Twenty-fifth Street in Manhattan, I saw the most beautiful photographs. "Hurrell?" I thought to myself. "Are these by Hurrell?" George Hurrell, for those of you who don't know, was the Hollywood photographer who took the classic movie-star pictures of the thirties, forties, and fifties, pictures that transcended and became works of art and collector's items. David Begelman, once the head of Columbia Pictures, whose career floundered after he forged a check for ten thousand dollars in the name of the actor Cliff Robertson, had a complete set of beautifully framed Hurrell photographs decorating the living room walls of his New York pied-à-terre. A later studio head, Peter Guber, who is no longer a studio head, has a complete set of beautifully framed Hurrell photographs on the walls of his yacht.

But of course the pictures I saw that day in Len Prince's studio weren't by Hurrell, and that wasn't really Jean Harlow in the picture. It was Drew Barrymore, looking like the epitome of a MGM star in black with ostrich feathers and a great many pearls, wonderfully lit, exuding glamour. The pictures were by Len Prince himself. We must have spent an hour looking through them, and we looked through them once again together at the Chateau Marmont in Hollywood a few months later. He said he wanted to do a book of them. I said I thought it was a wonderful idea. He said, not then, but later, "Would you consider writing an introduction?" I of course said yes. This is it. What a treat you have in store.   DOMINICK DUNNE 1997

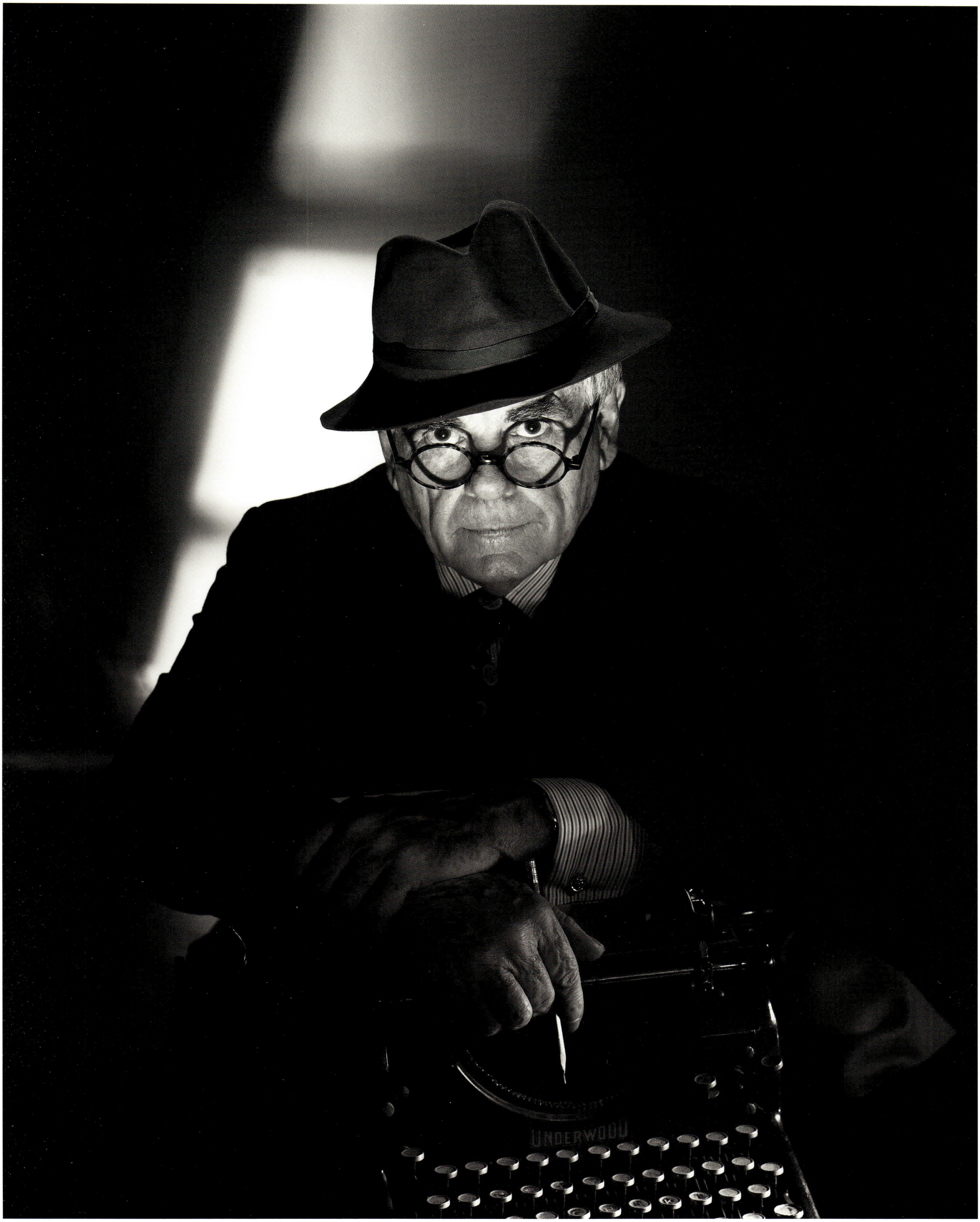
UNDERWOOD

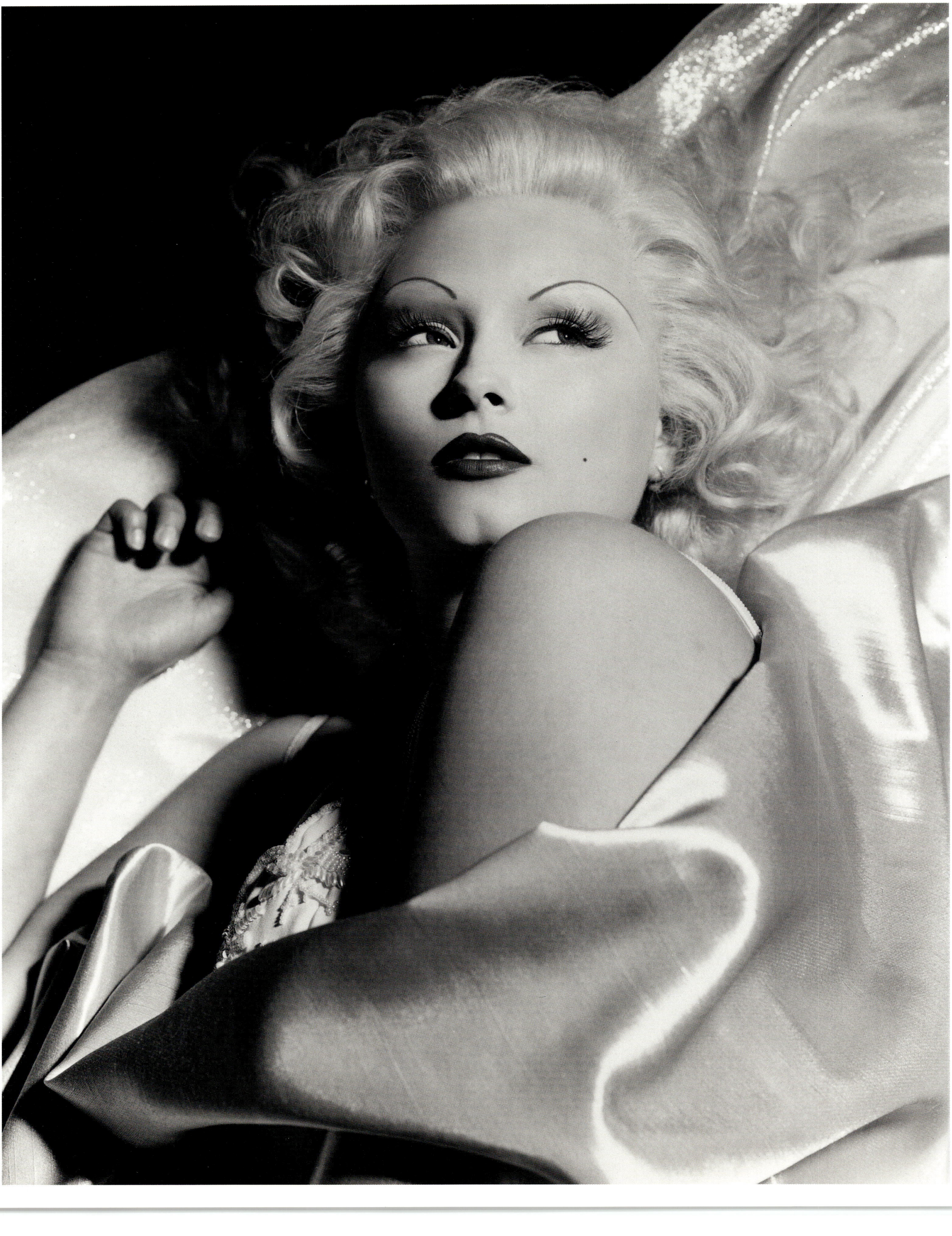

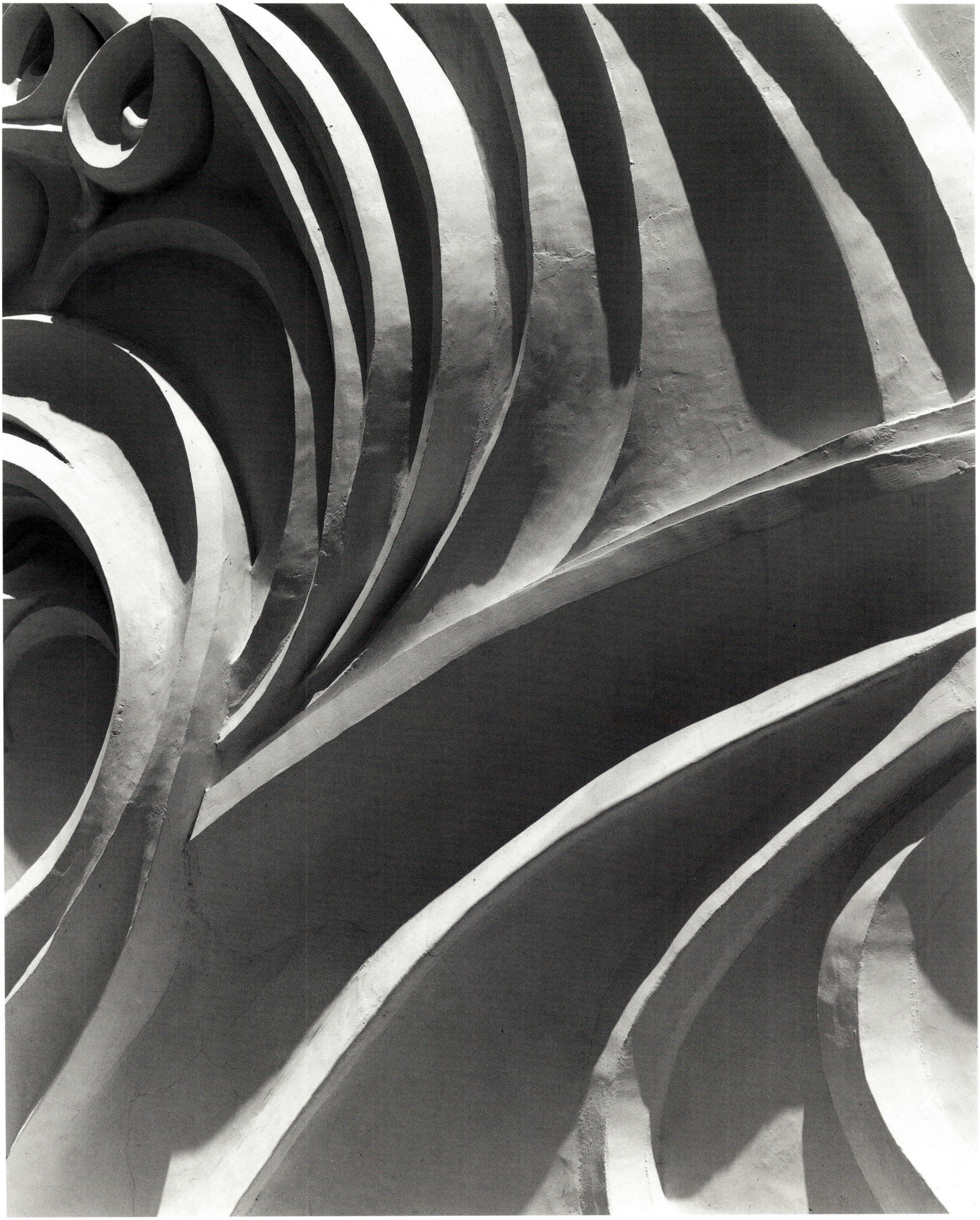

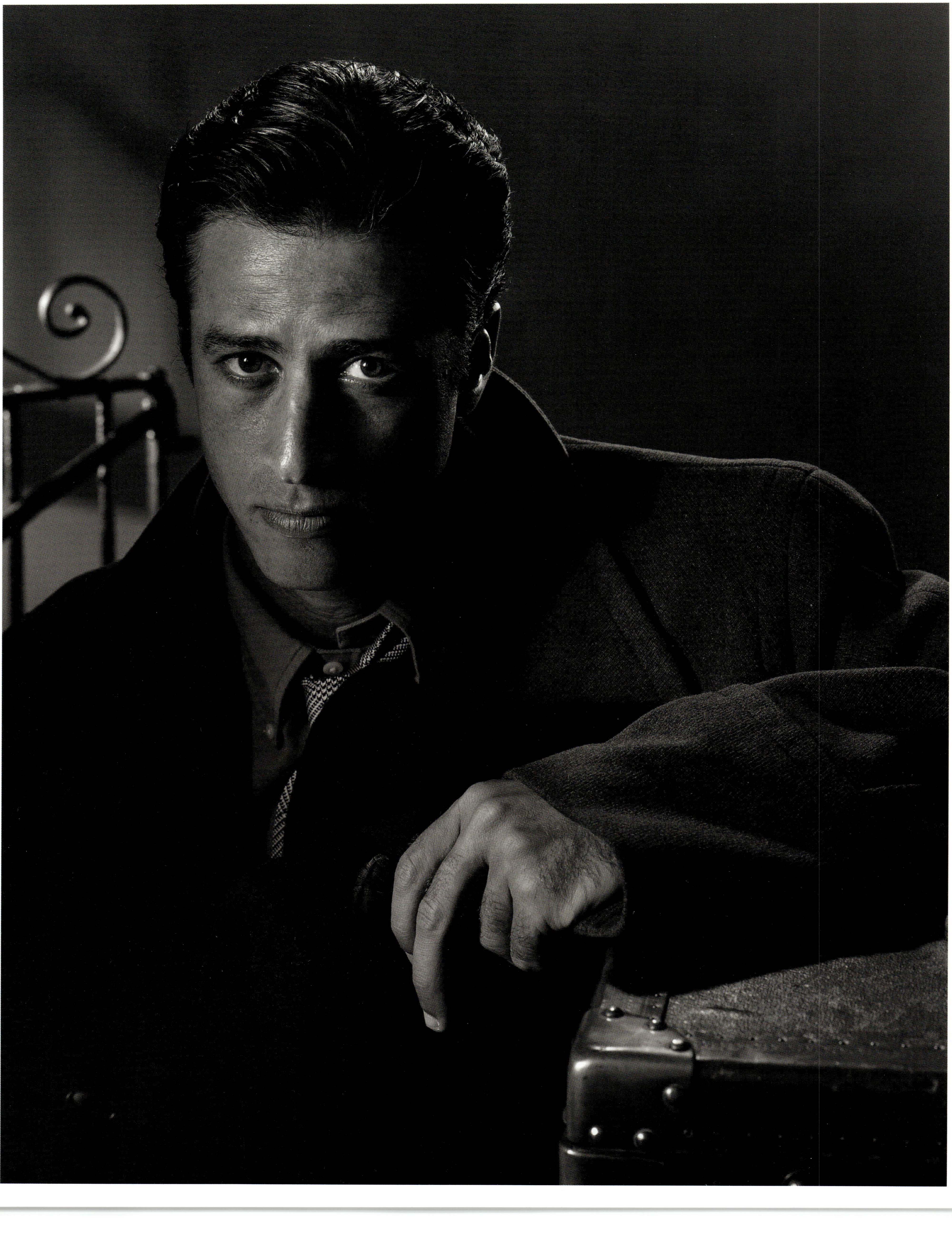

PRECEDING PAGES:

LEFT: NINA SIEMASZKO, CHATEAU MARMONT, HOLLYWOOD, 1994

RIGHT: PLASTER NOUVEAU DETAIL II, BEVERLY HILLS, 1994

JOHN STEWART, NEW YORK CITY, 1996

MARTIN SHEEN, STUDIO 70/70 A, SANTA MONICA BOULEVARD, 1995

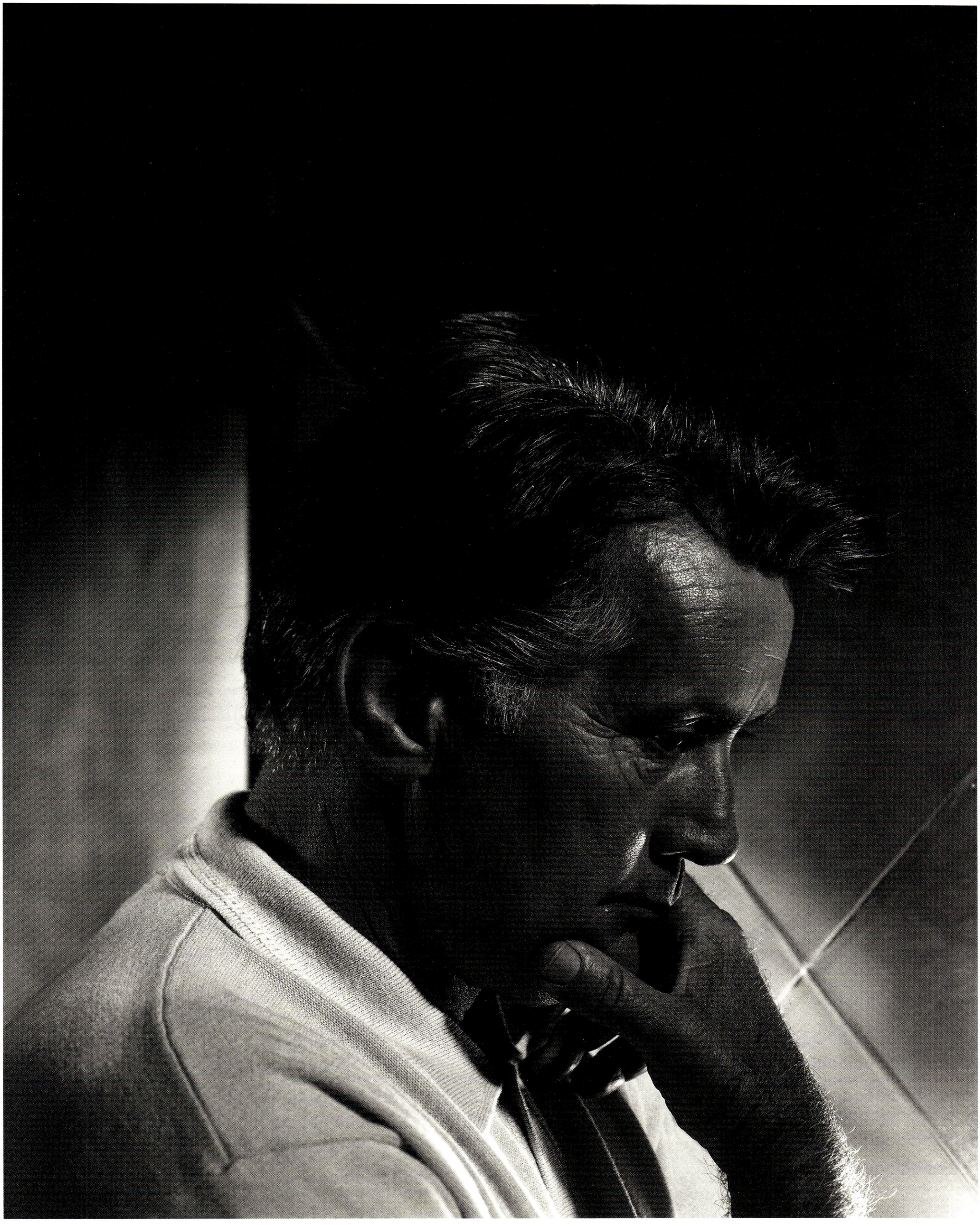

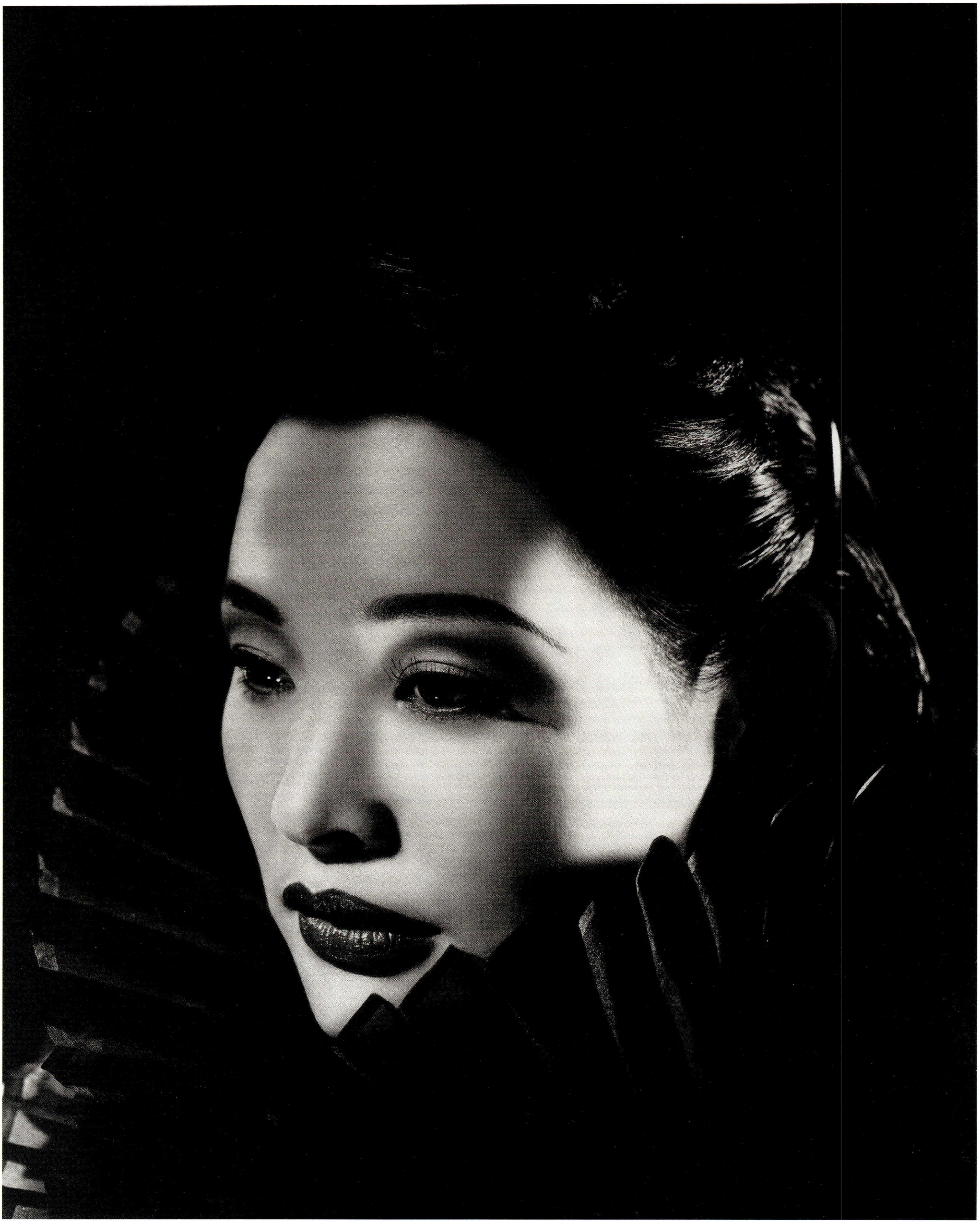

JOAN CHEN, STUDIO 70/70 A, SANTA MONICA BOULEVARD, 1994

MARGARET CHO, STUDIO 70/70 C, HOLLYWOOD, 1995

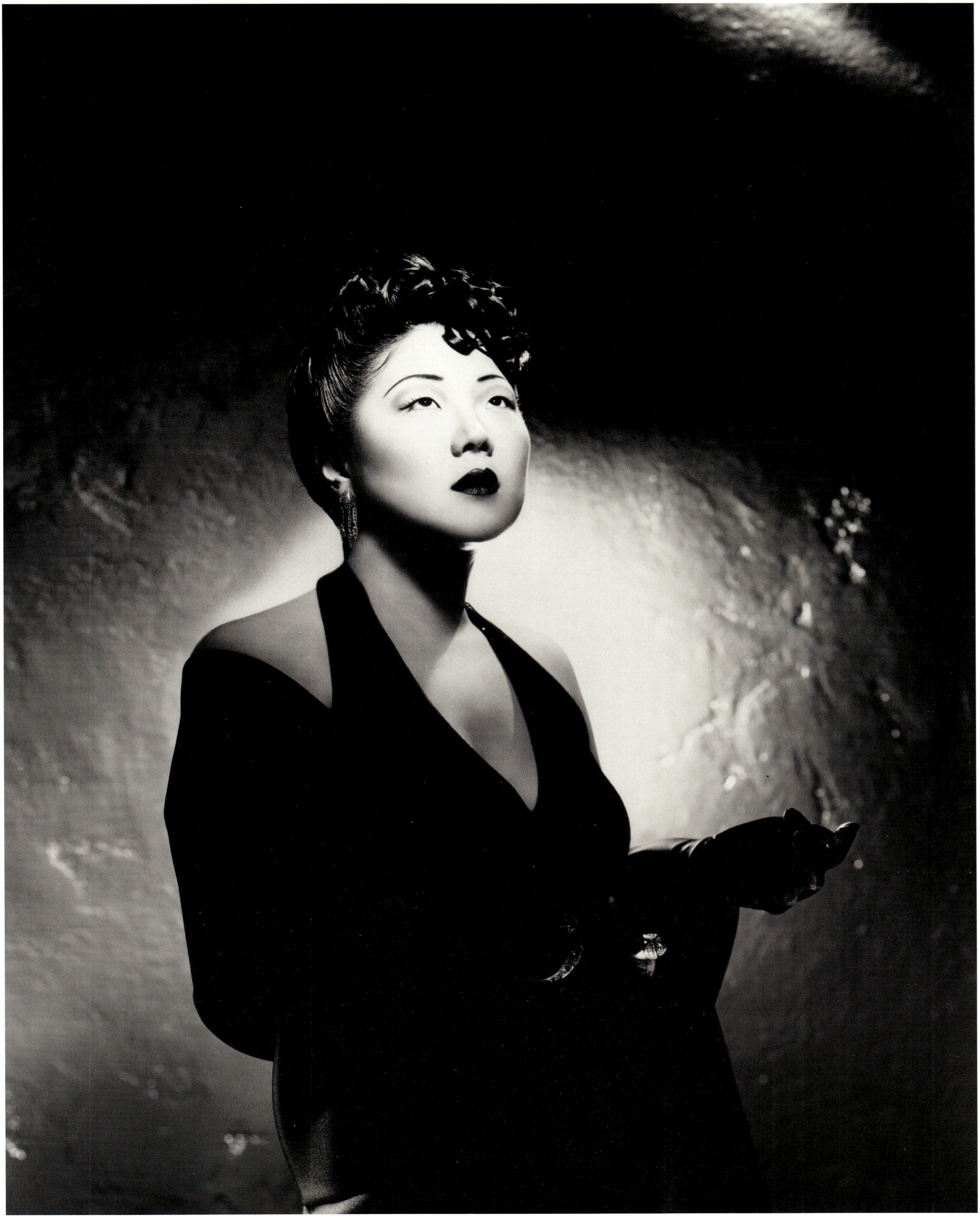

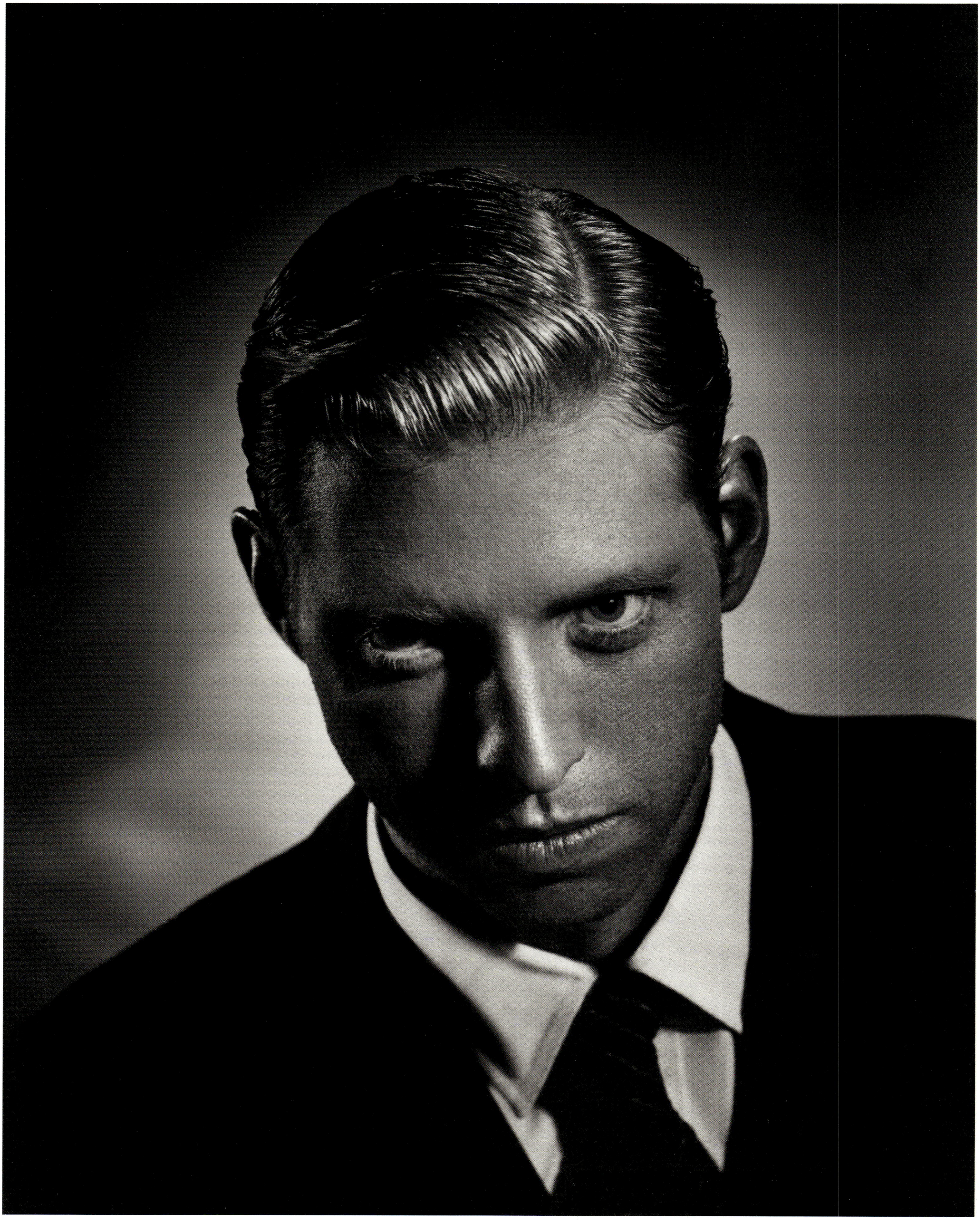

MATTHEW TYRNAUER, NEW YORK CITY, 1996

JULIANNE PHILLIPS, STUDIO 70/70 A, SANTA MONICA BOULEVARD, 1994

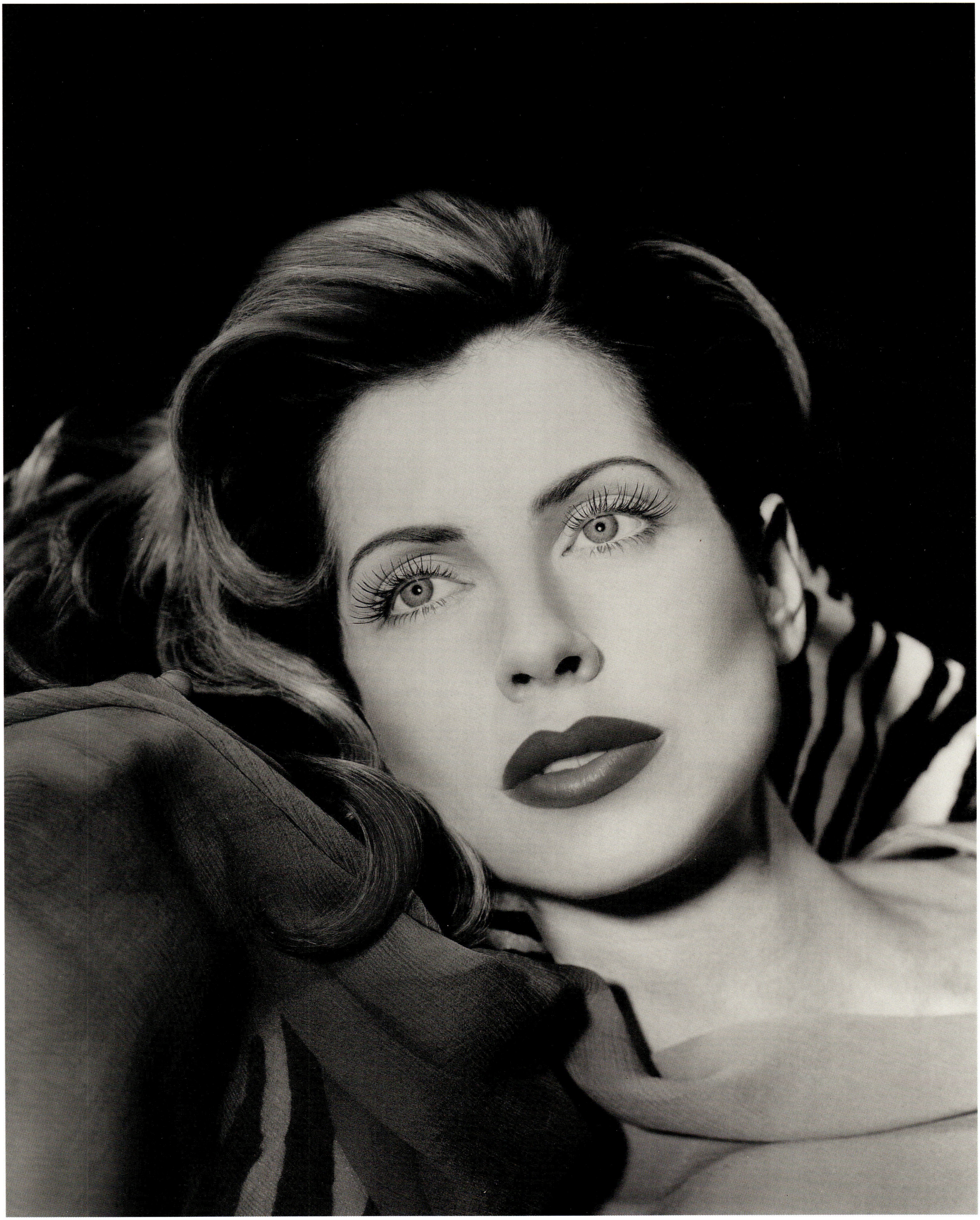

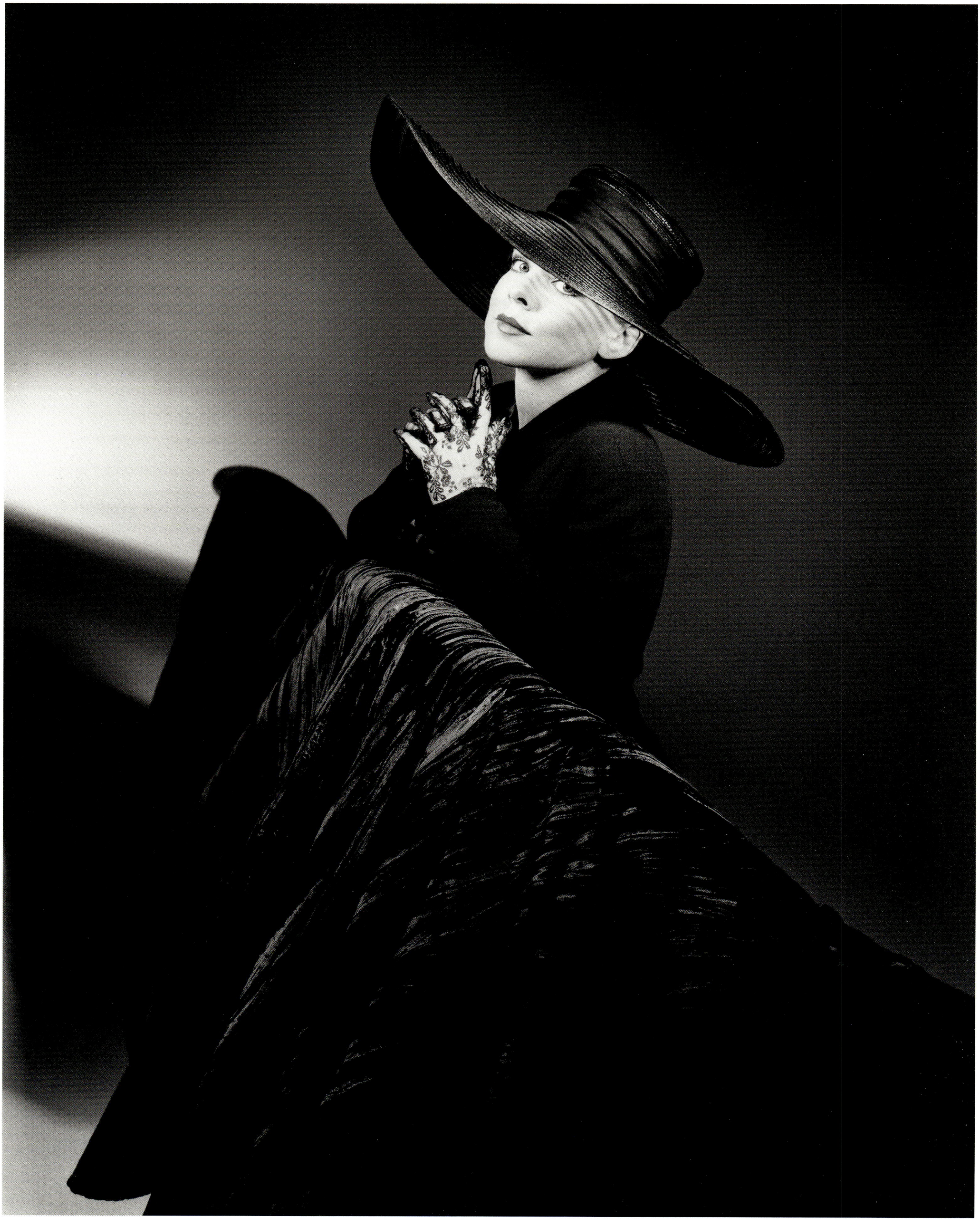

STOCKARD CHANNING, STUDIO 70/70 A, SANTA MONICA BOULEVARD, 1994

EVANDER HOLYFIELD, NEW YORK CITY, 1997

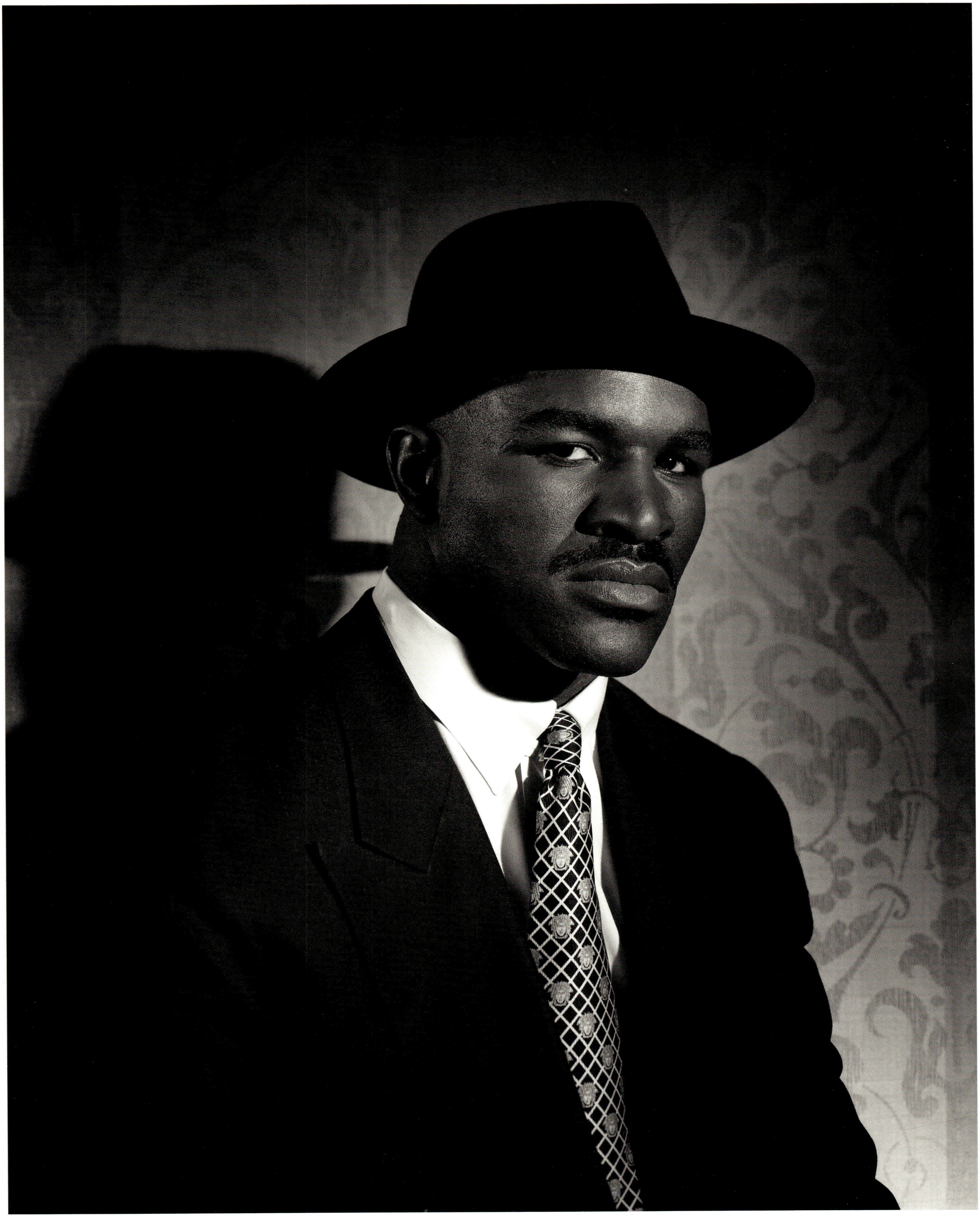

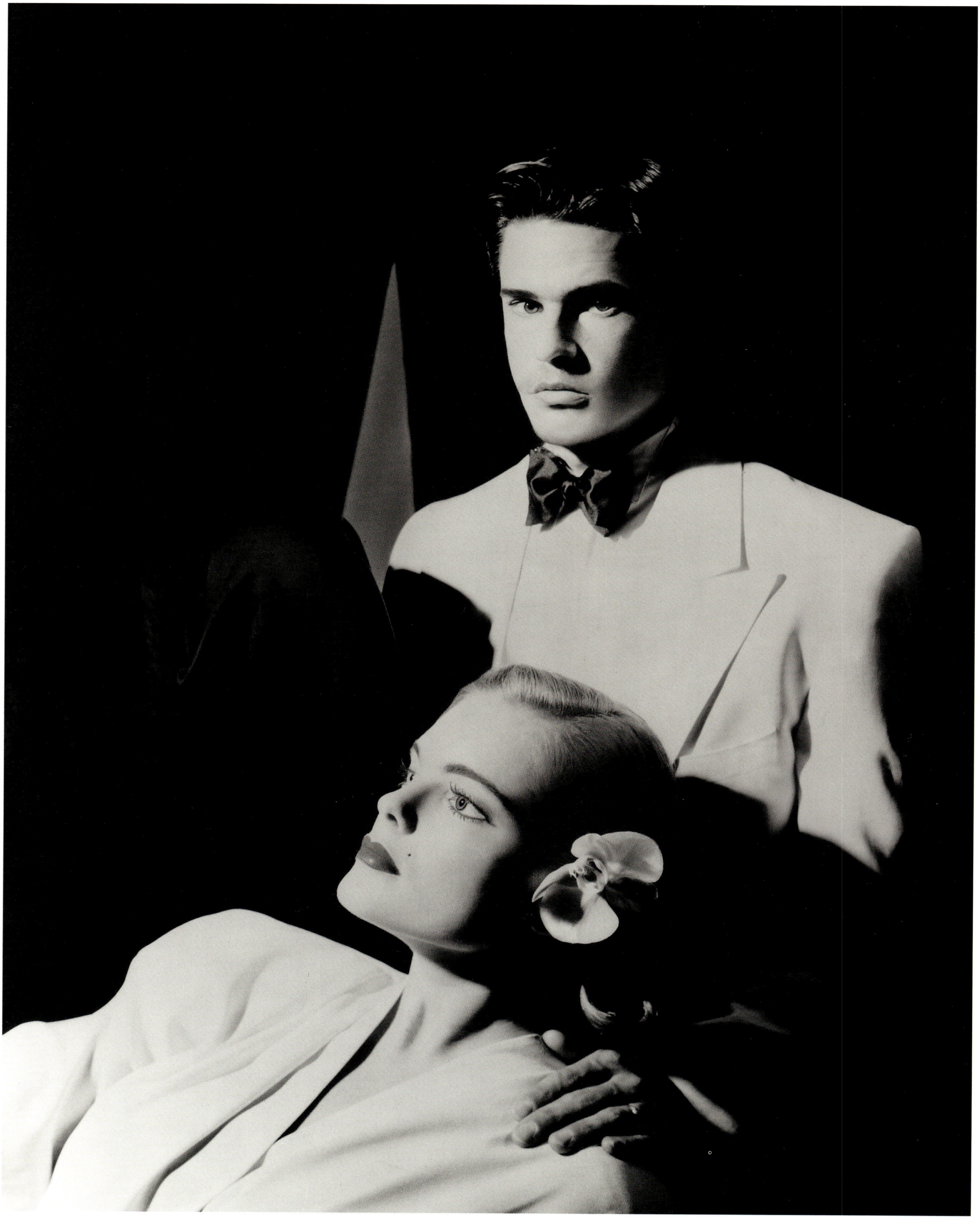

WILLIAM MCNAMARA AND ERIKA ELENIAK, CHATEAU MARMONT, HOLLYWOOD, 1994

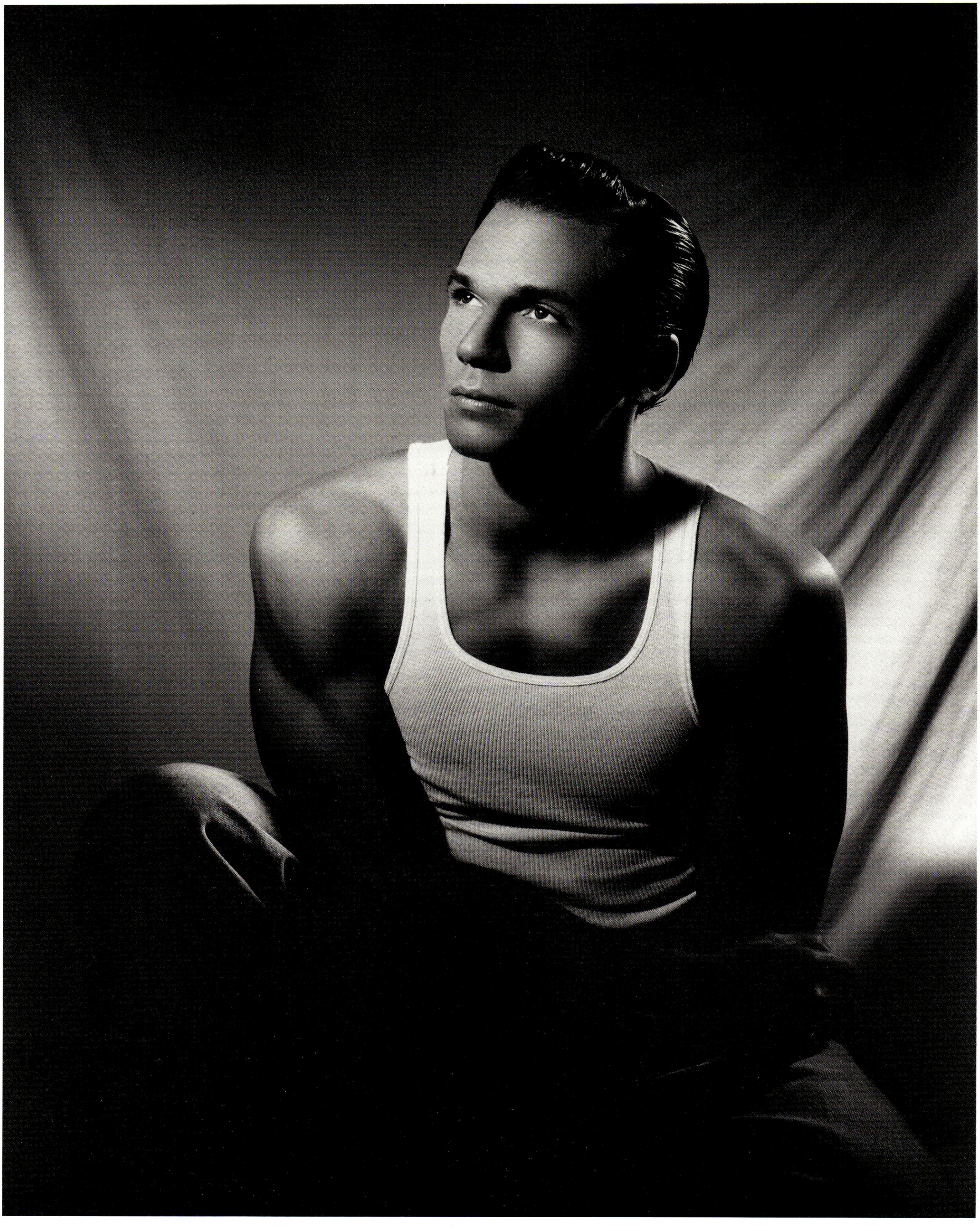

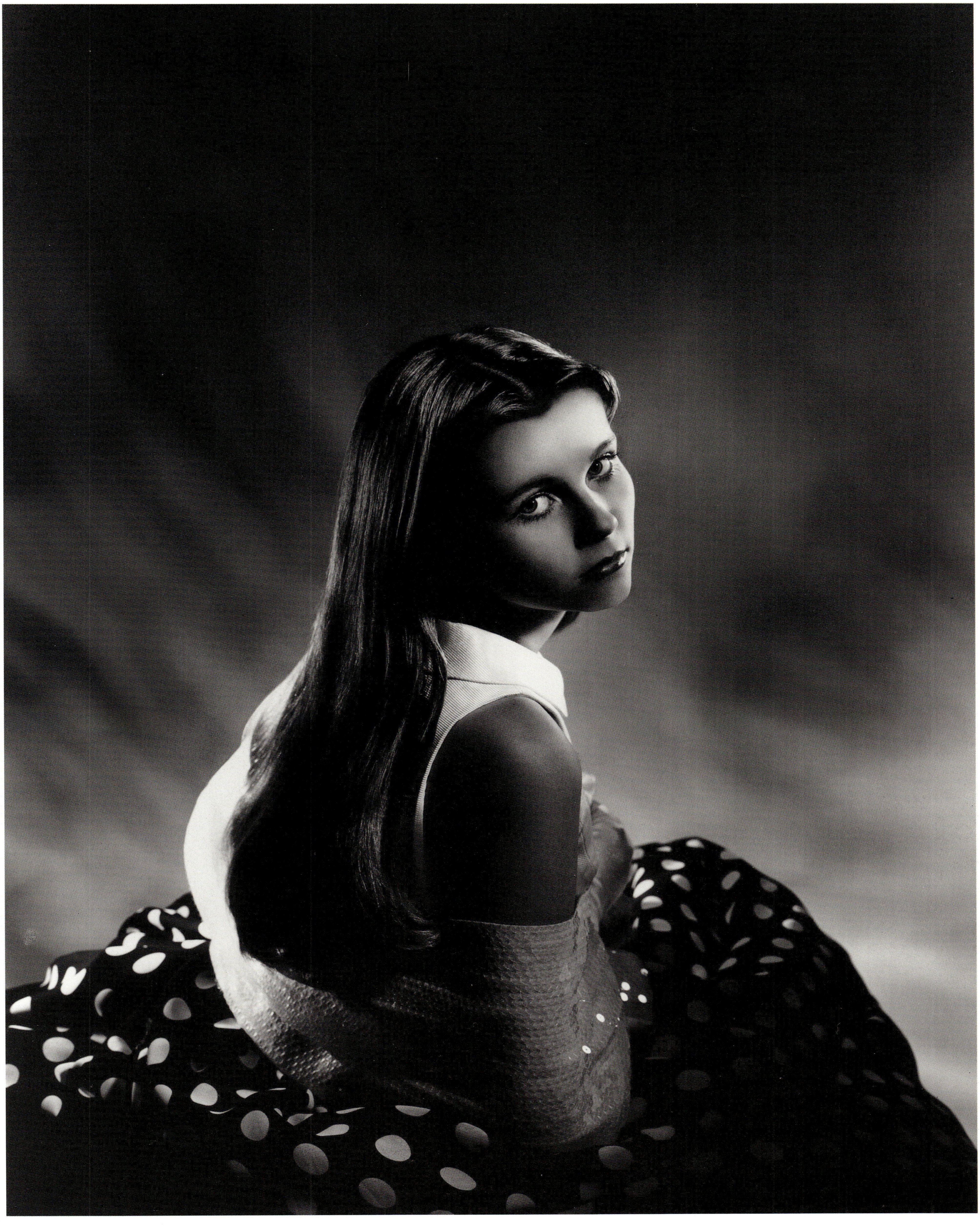

PRECEDING PAGES:

LEFT: ERIC THAL, CHATEAU MARMONT, HOLLYWOOD, 1994

RIGHT: KIRSTEN DUNST, STUDIO 70/70 C, HOLLYWOOD, 1995

TERI HATCHER AND JON TENNEY, STUDIO 70/70 C, HOLLYWOOD, 1994

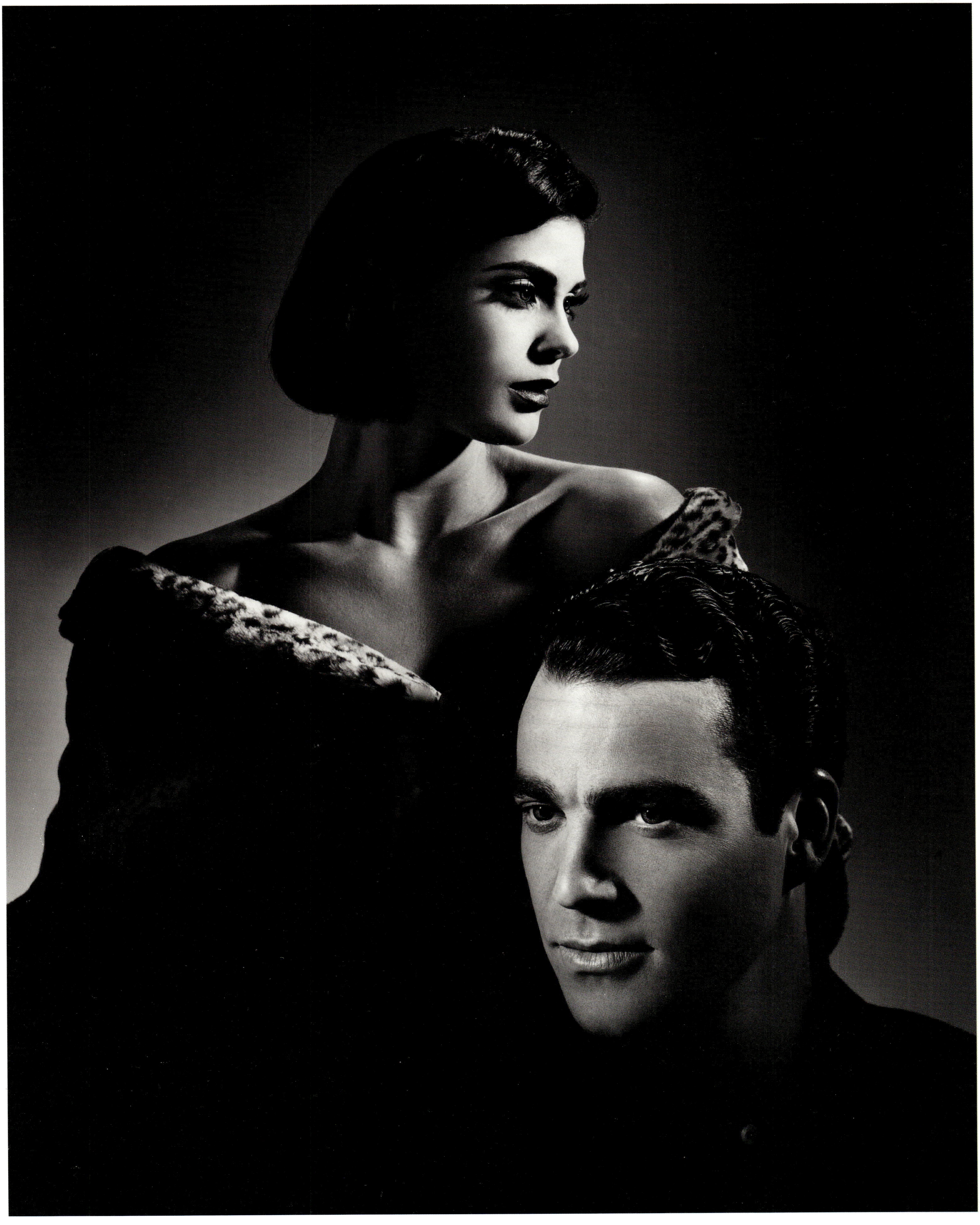

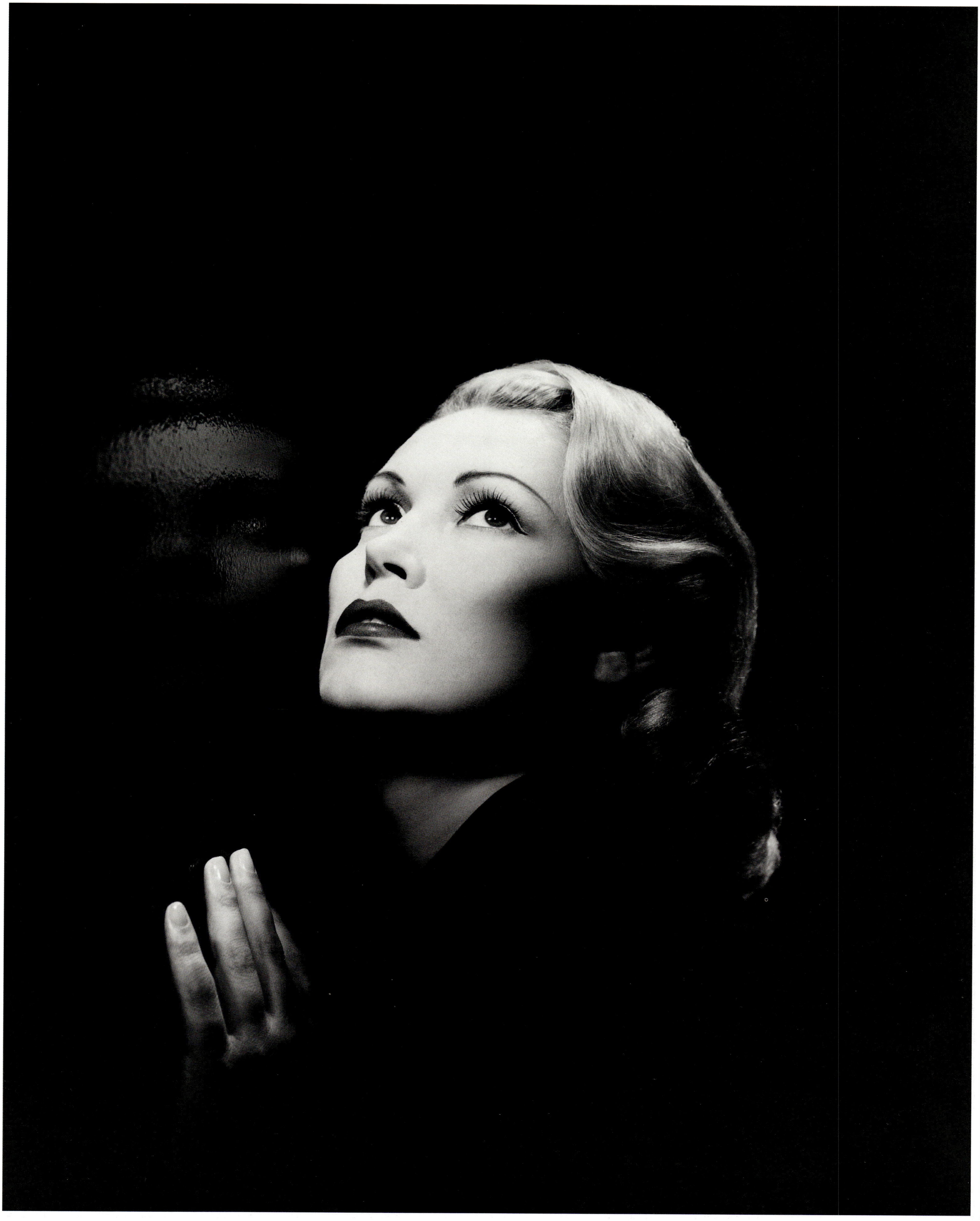

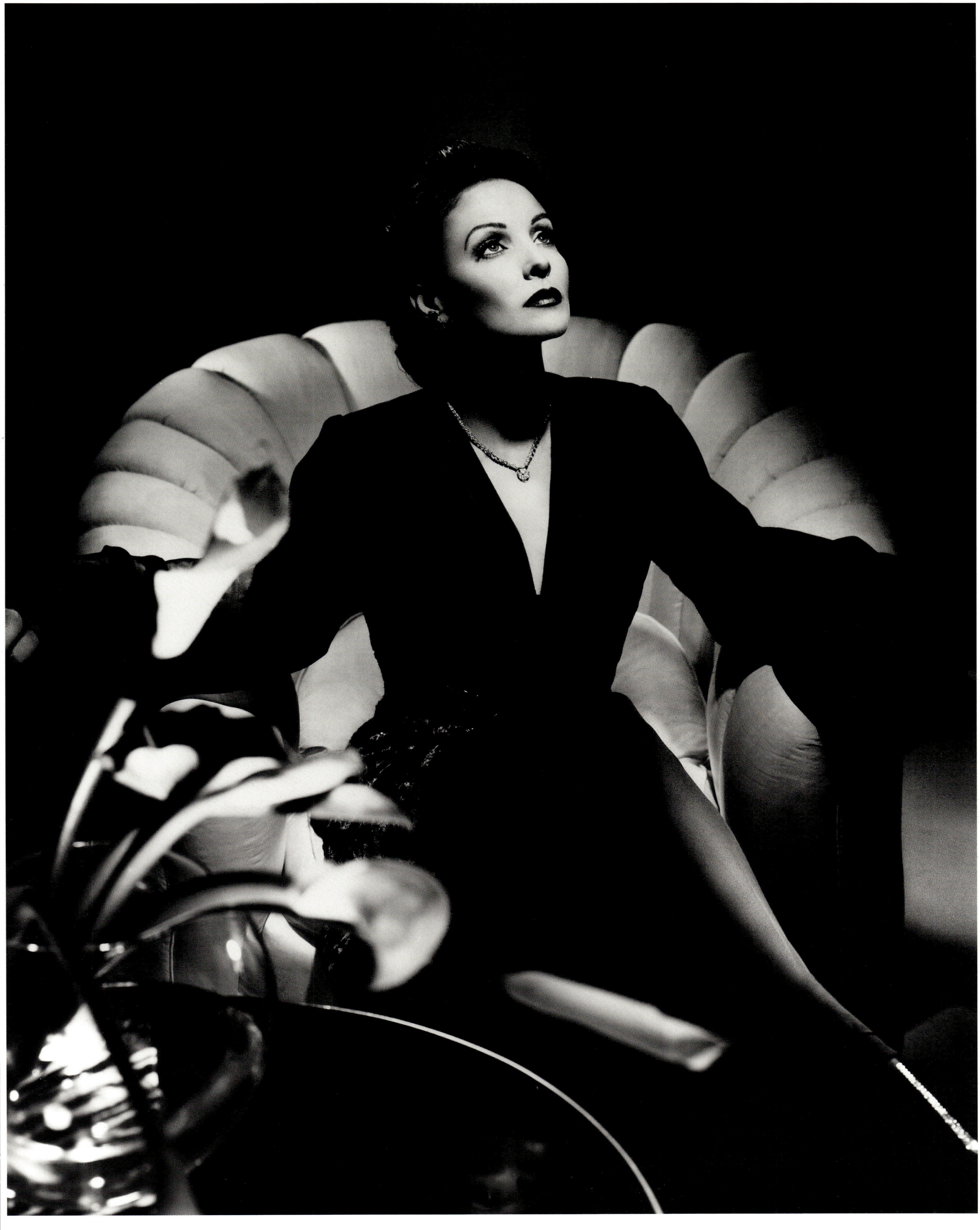

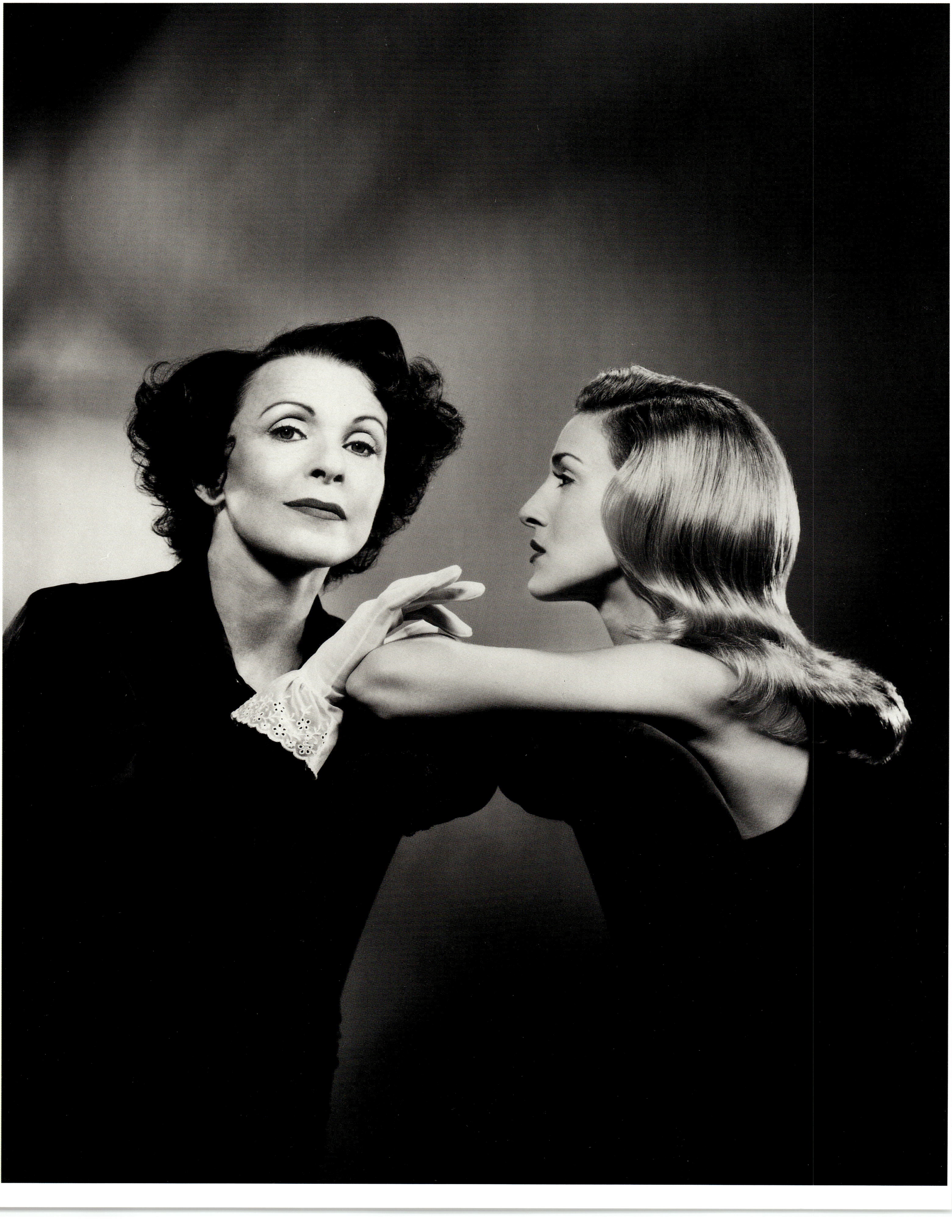

PRECEDING PAGES:

LEFT: CATHY MORIARTY, STUDIO 70/70 B, SANTA MONICA BOULEVARD, 1994

RIGHT: KATHLEEN QUINLAN, STUDIO 70/70 C, HOLLYWOOD, 1995

CLAIRE BLOOM AND SARAH JESSICA PARKER, NEW YORK CITY, 1995

LAUREN HOLLY, CHATEAU MARMONT, HOLLYWOOD, 1994

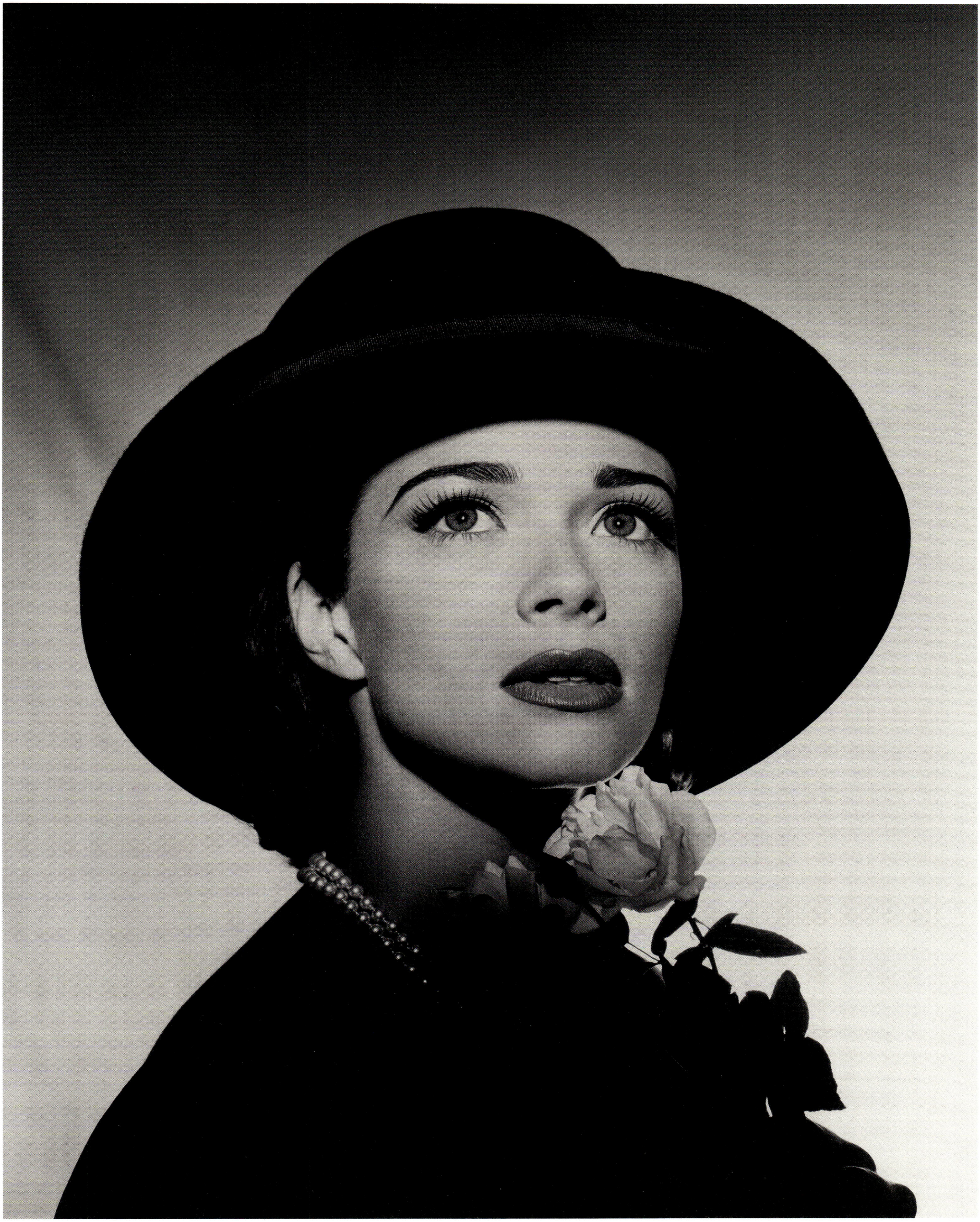

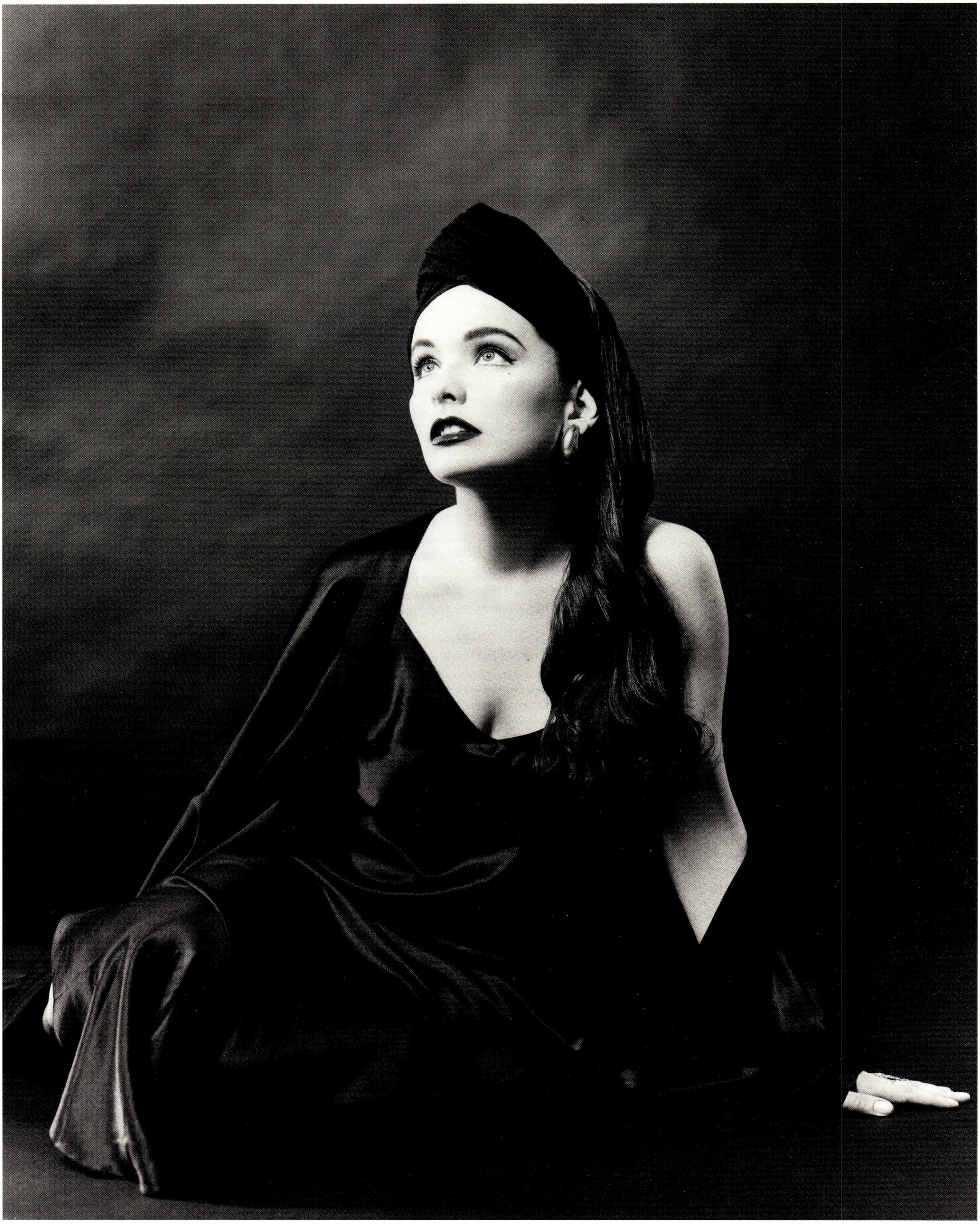

GUINEVERE TURNER, NEW YORK CITY, 1994

BEVERLY JOHNSON, STUDIO 70/70 B, SANTA MONICA BOULEVARD, 1994

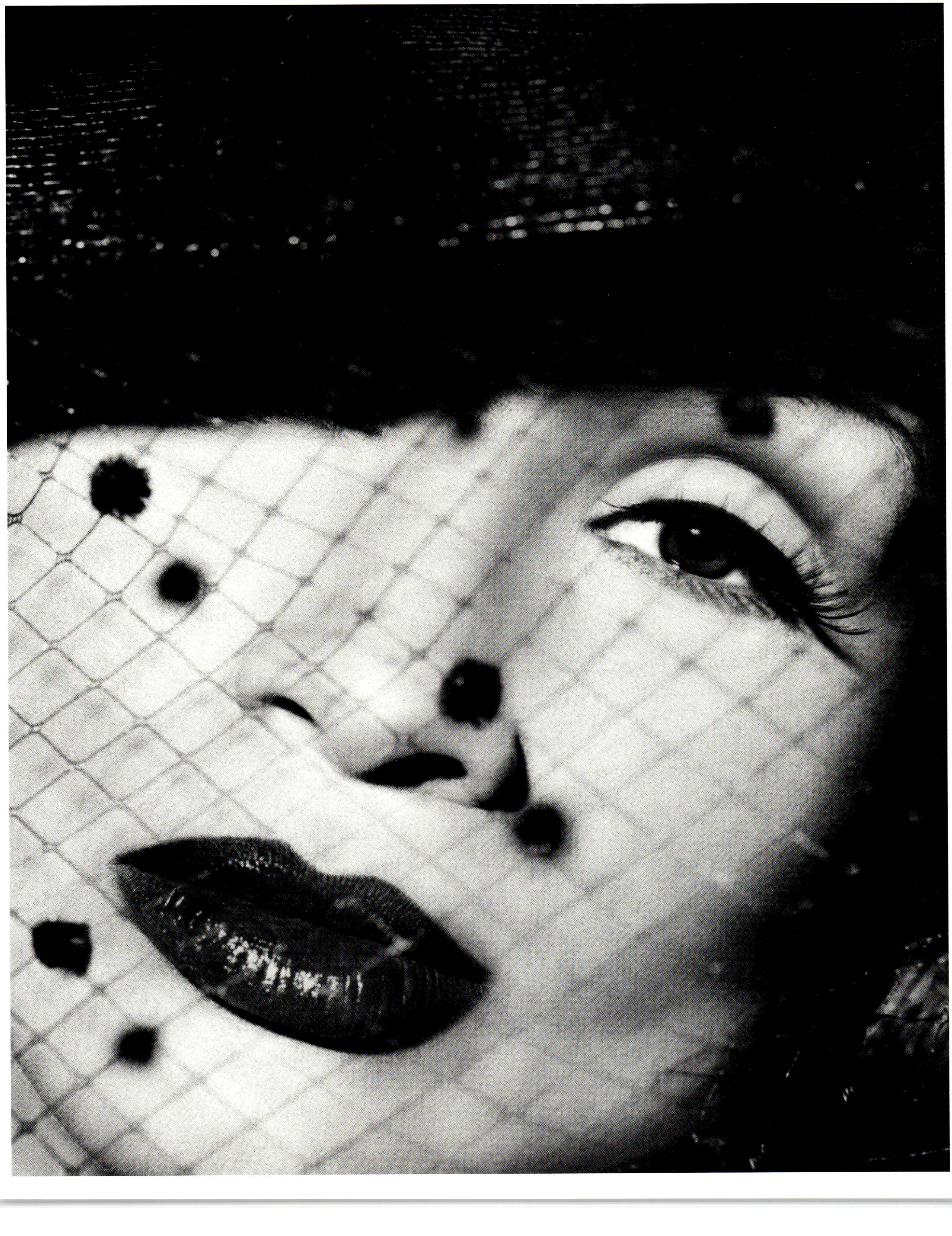

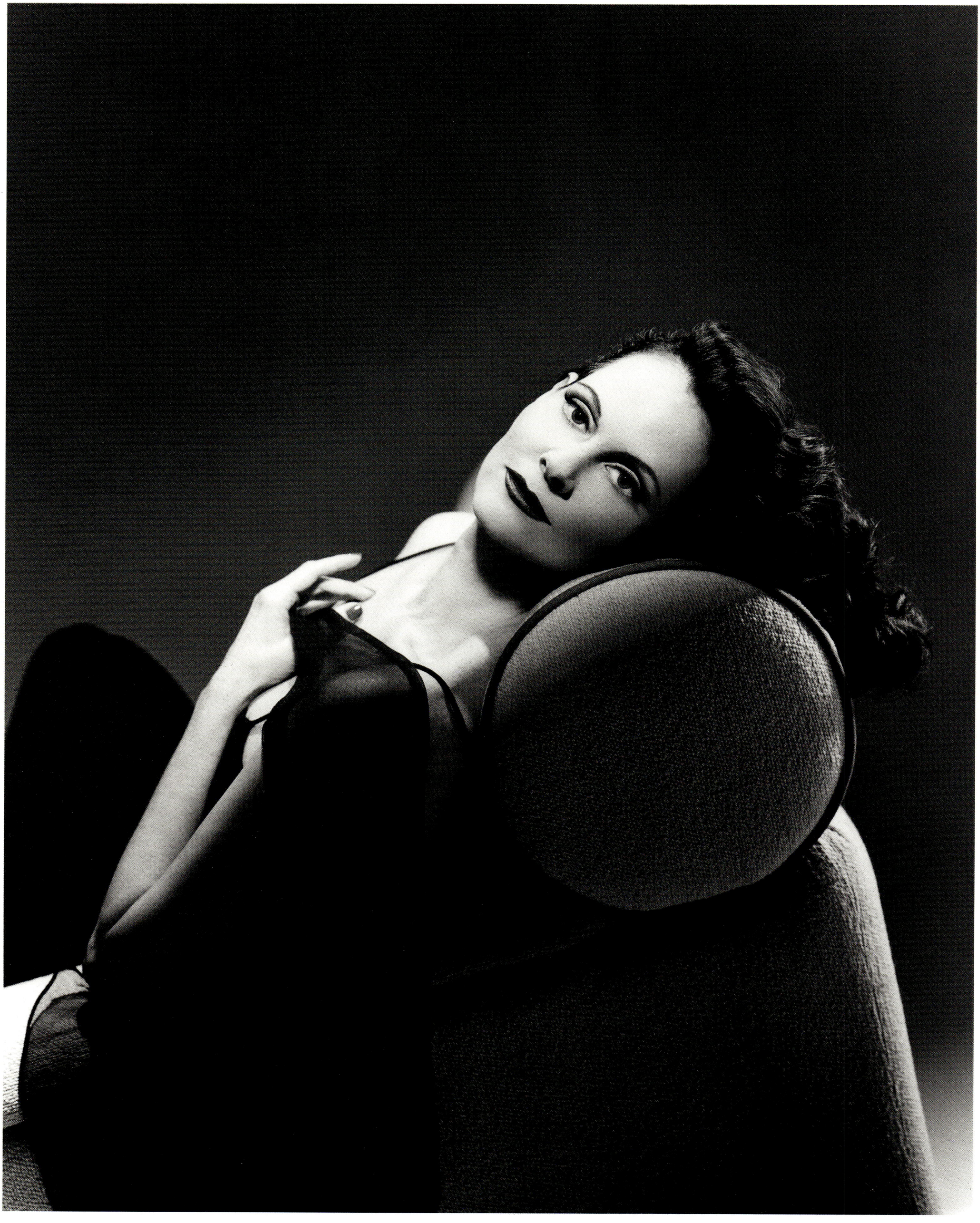

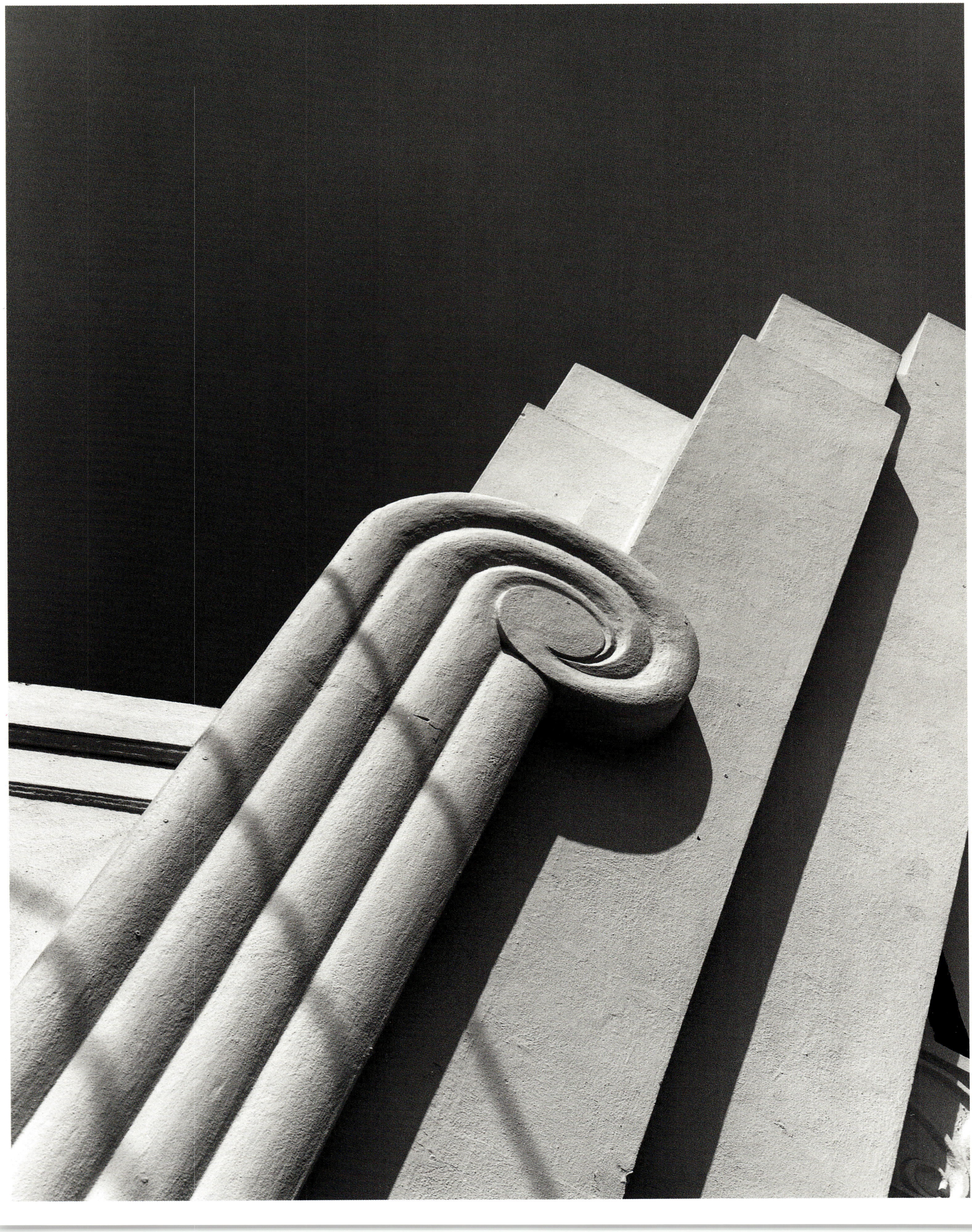

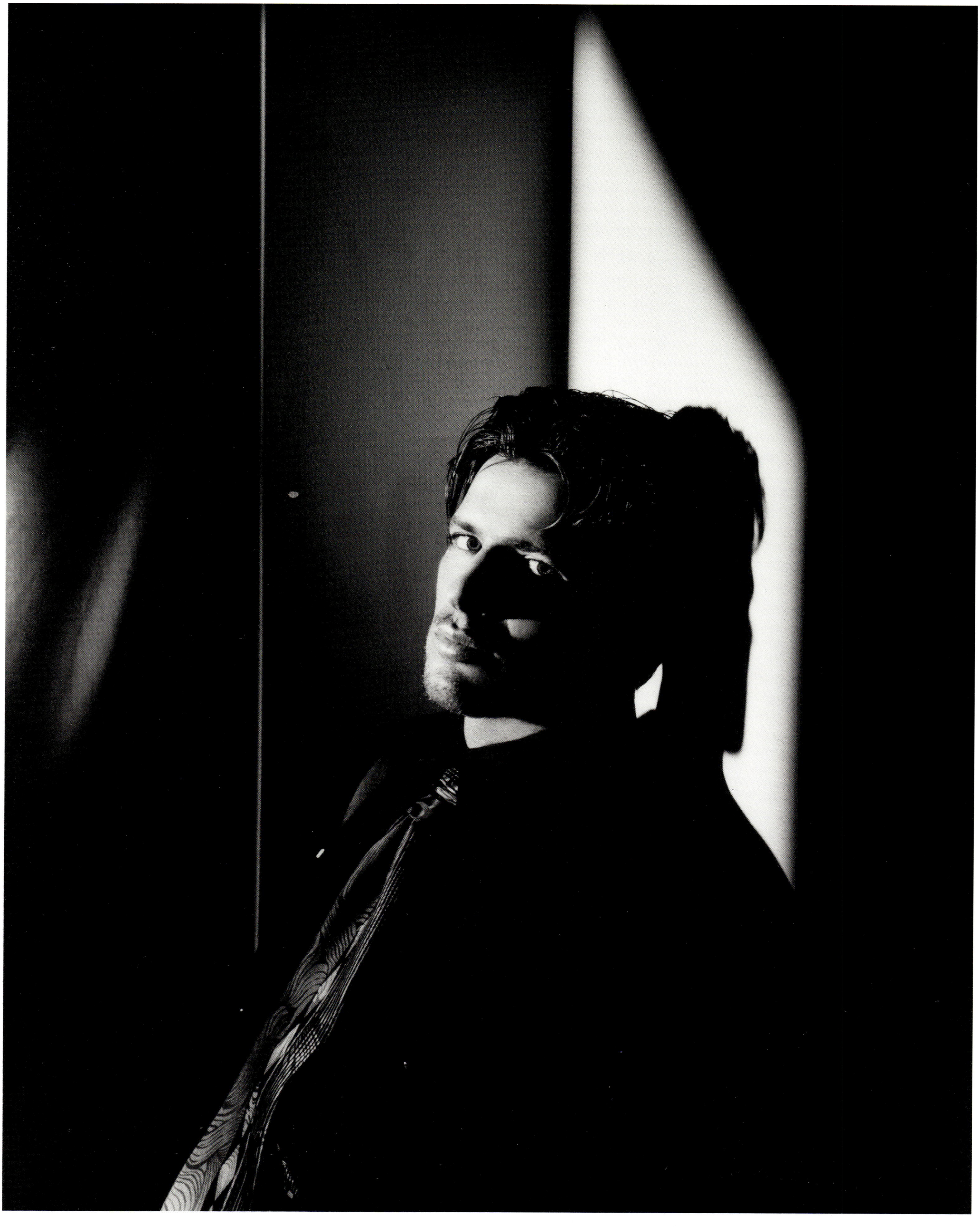

PRECEDING PAGES:

LEFT: LESLEY ANN WARREN, SANTA MONICA BOULEVARD, 1994

RIGHT: BUILDING DETAIL NO. 1, MELROSE AVENUE, HOLLYWOOD, 1995

COSTAS MANDYLOR, CHATEAU MARMONT, HOLLYWOOD, 1994

ILLEANA DOUGLAS, NEW YORK CITY, 1996

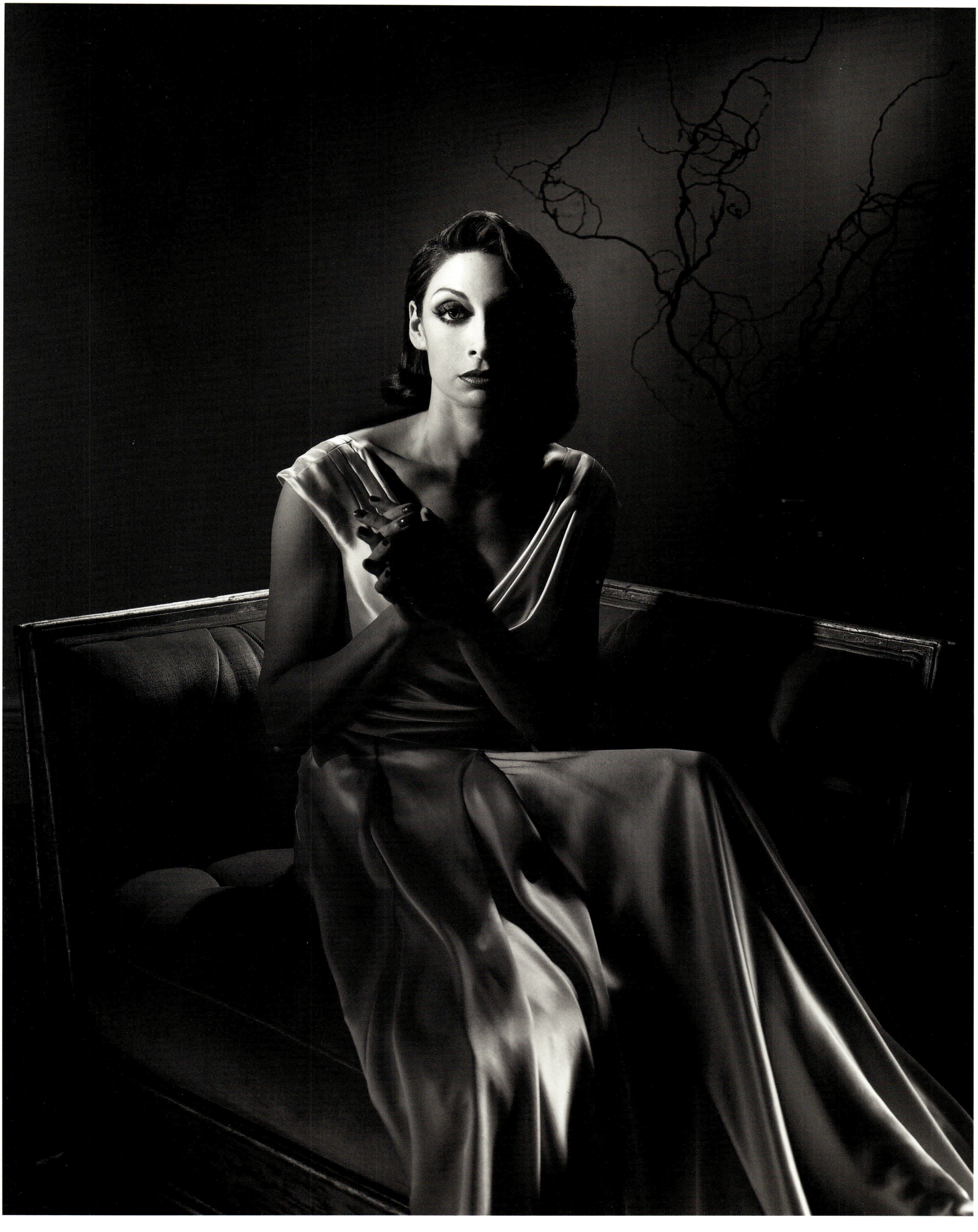

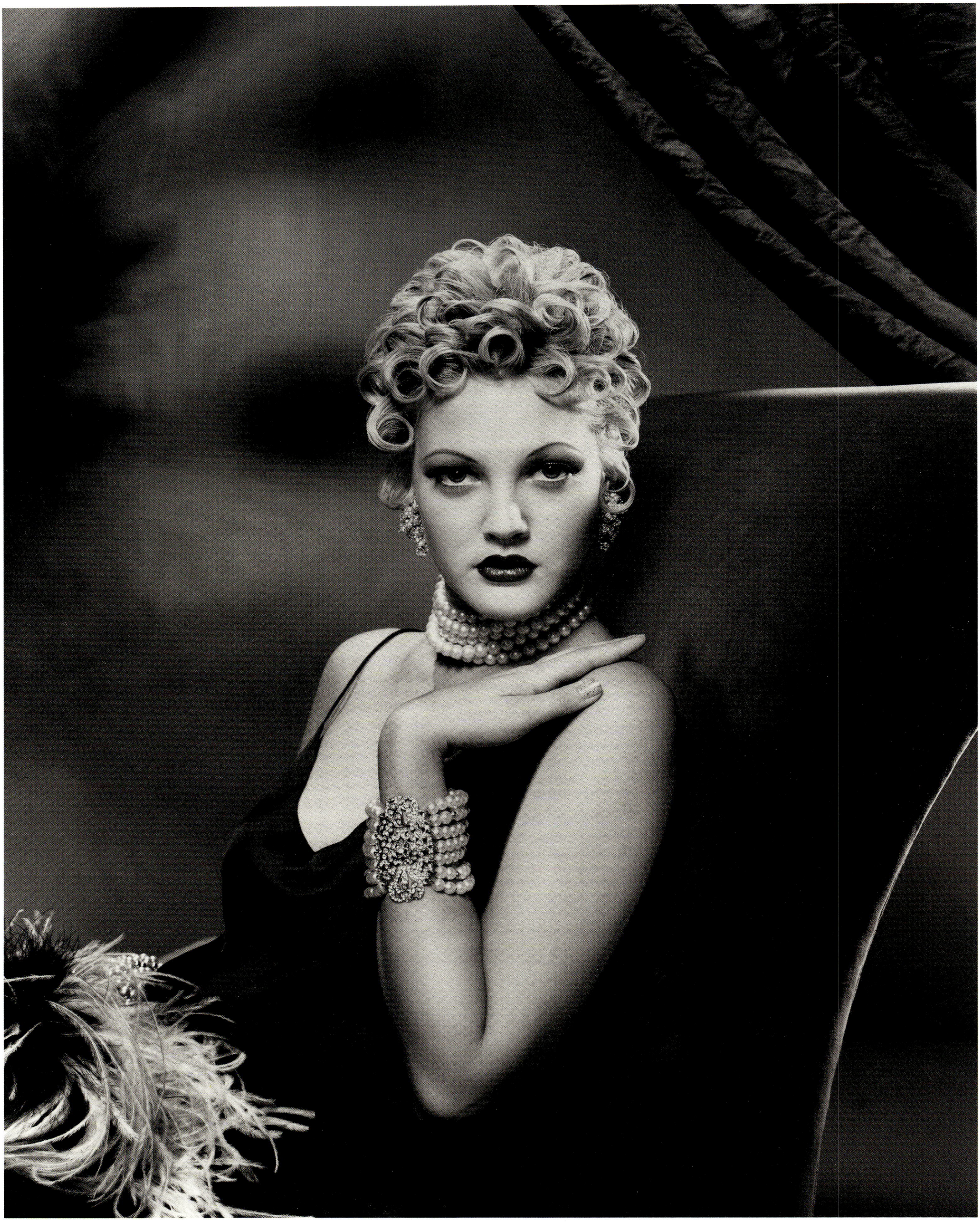

DREW BARRYMORE, NEW YORK CITY, 1994

ANN MAGNUSON, UNION STATION, LOS ANGELES, 1994

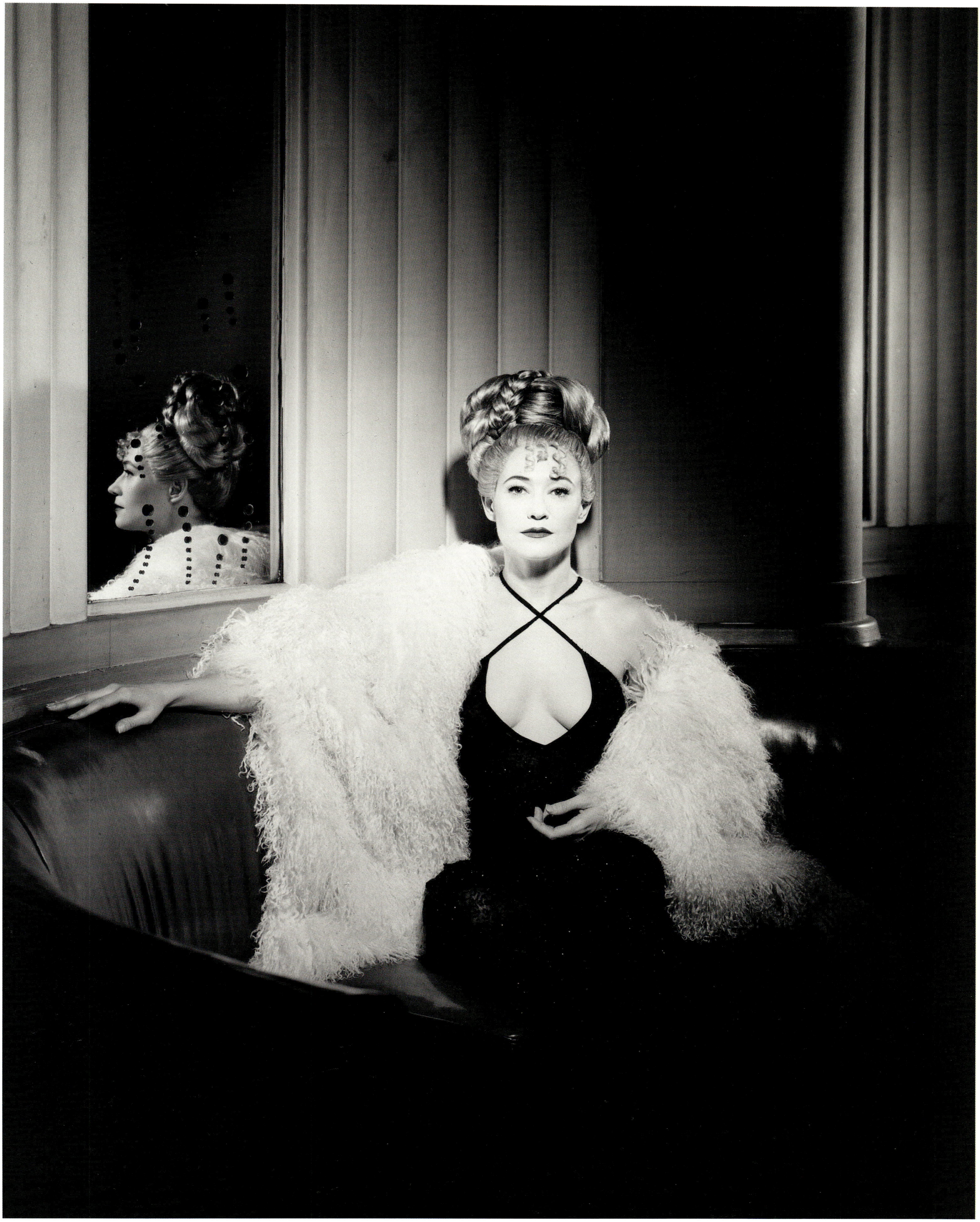

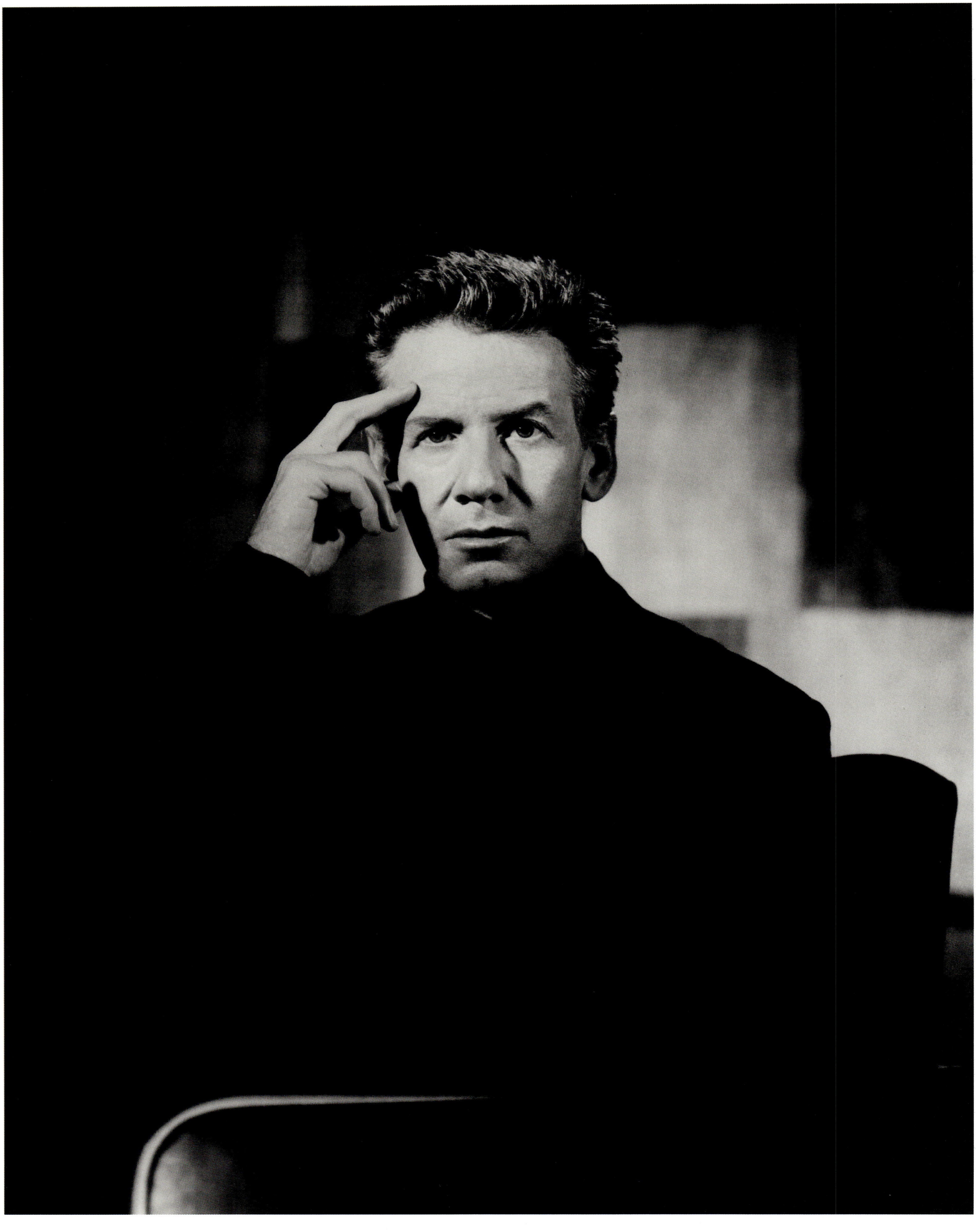

CALVIN KLEIN, PIER 59 STUDIO, NEW YORK CITY, 1996

PETER HORTON, STUDIO 70/70 C, HOLLYWOOD, 1995

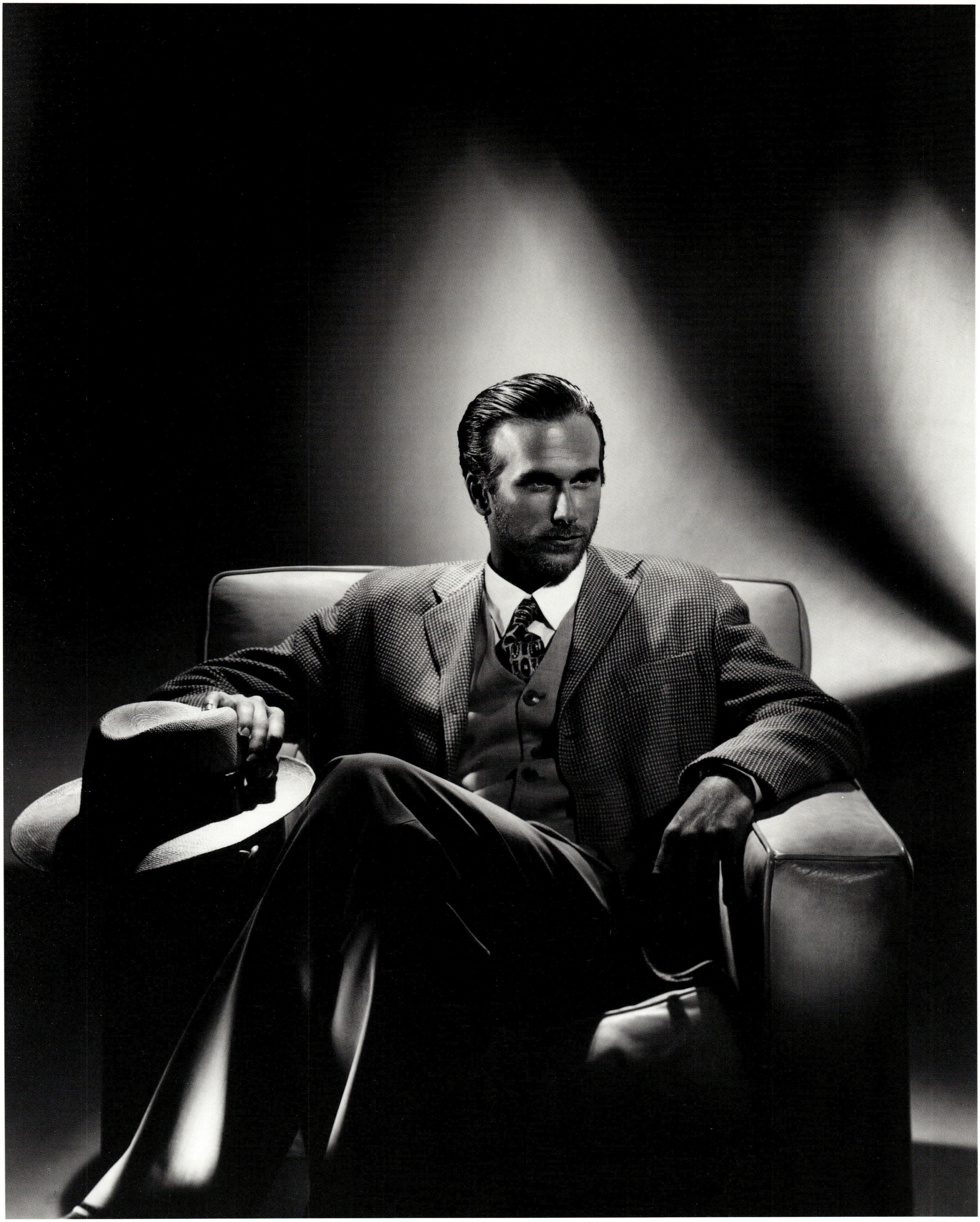

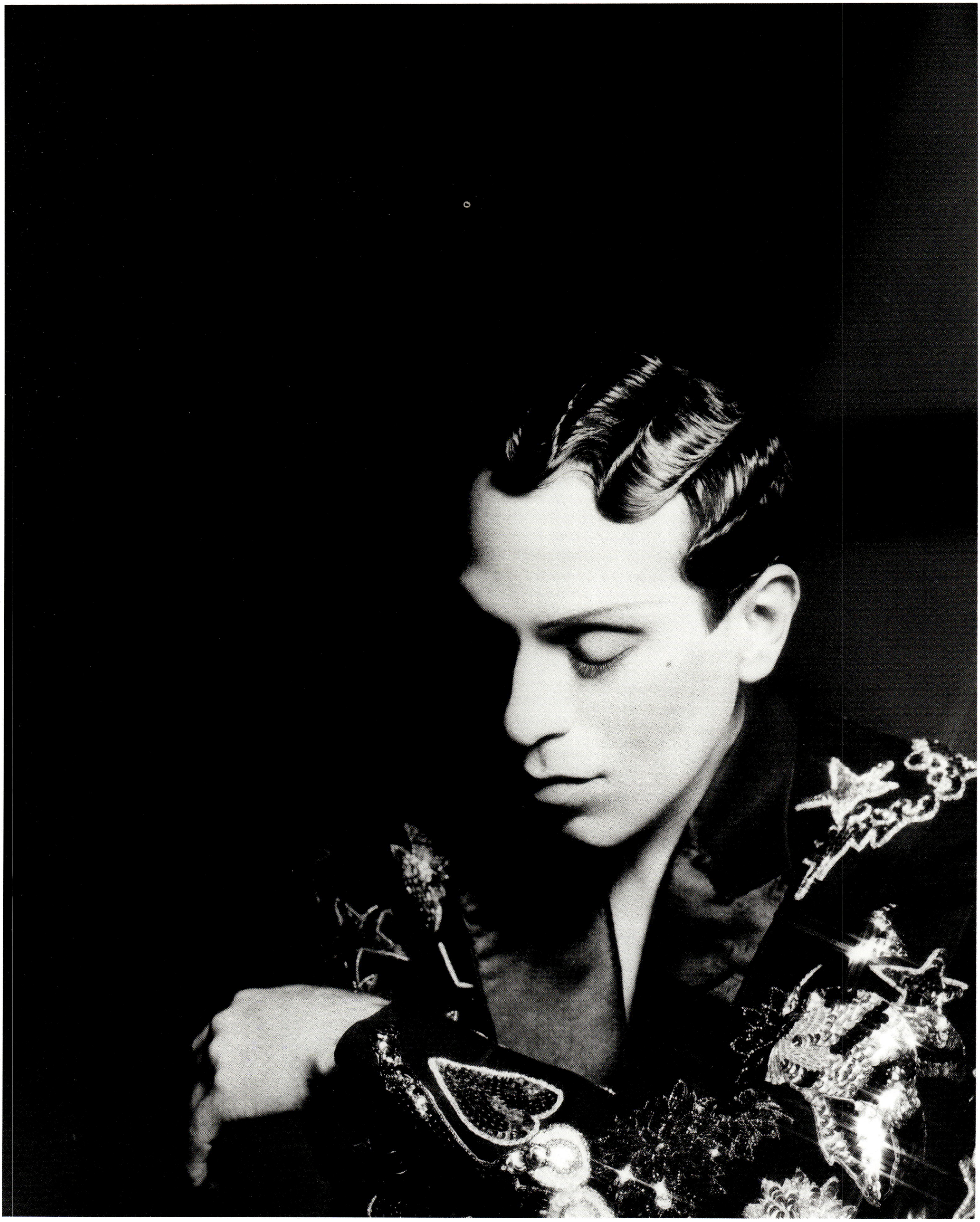

JOEY ARIAS, NEW YORK CITY, 1993

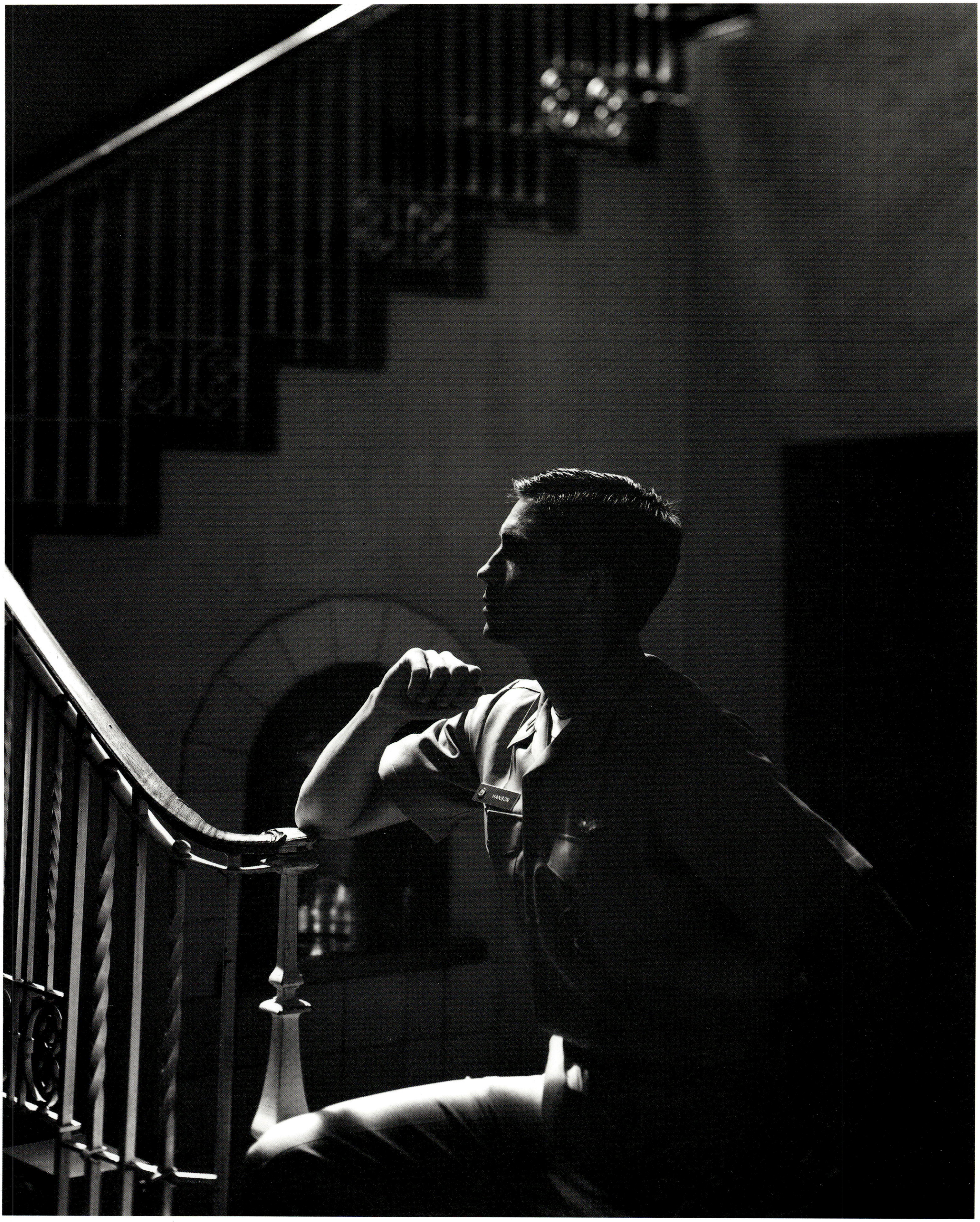

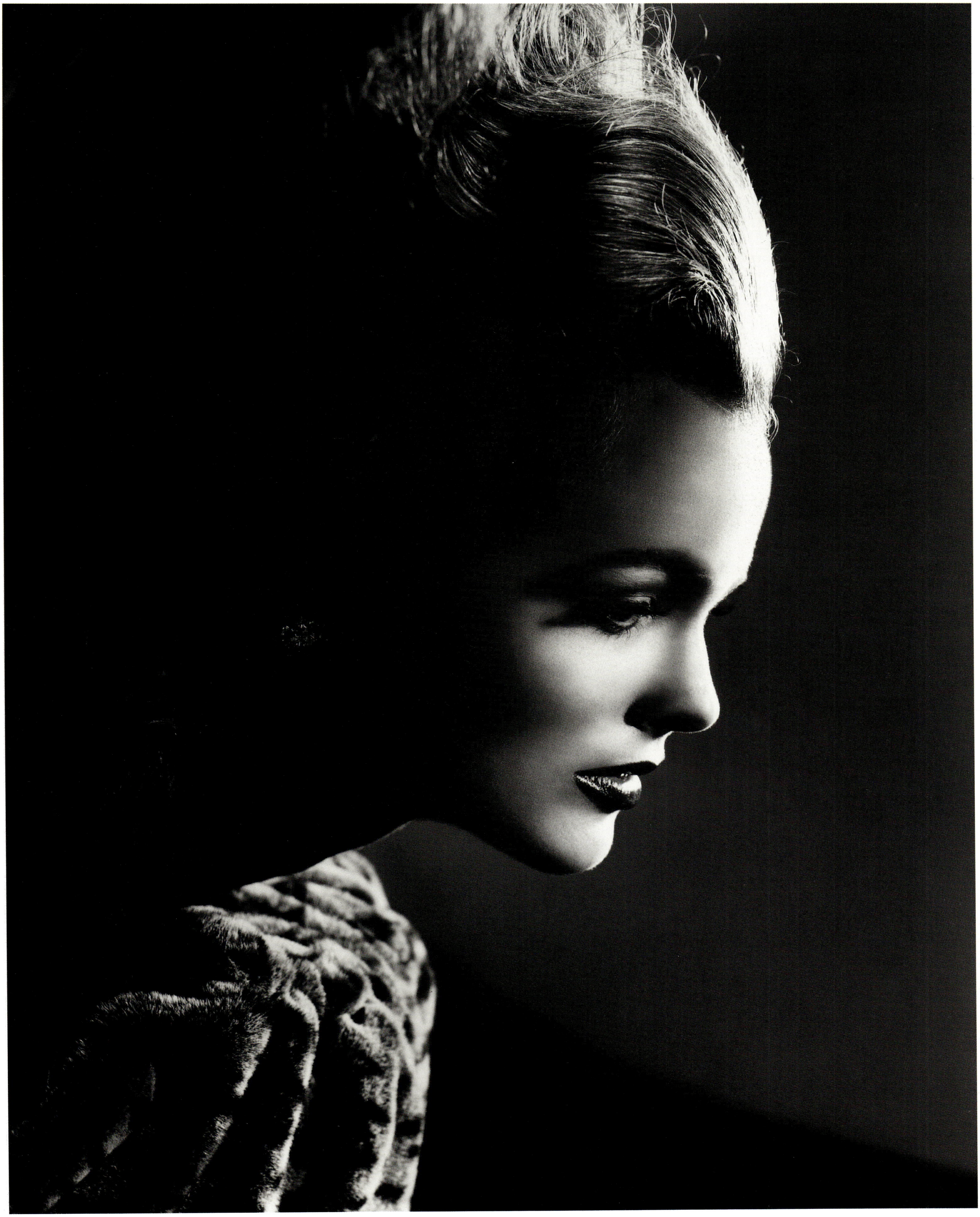

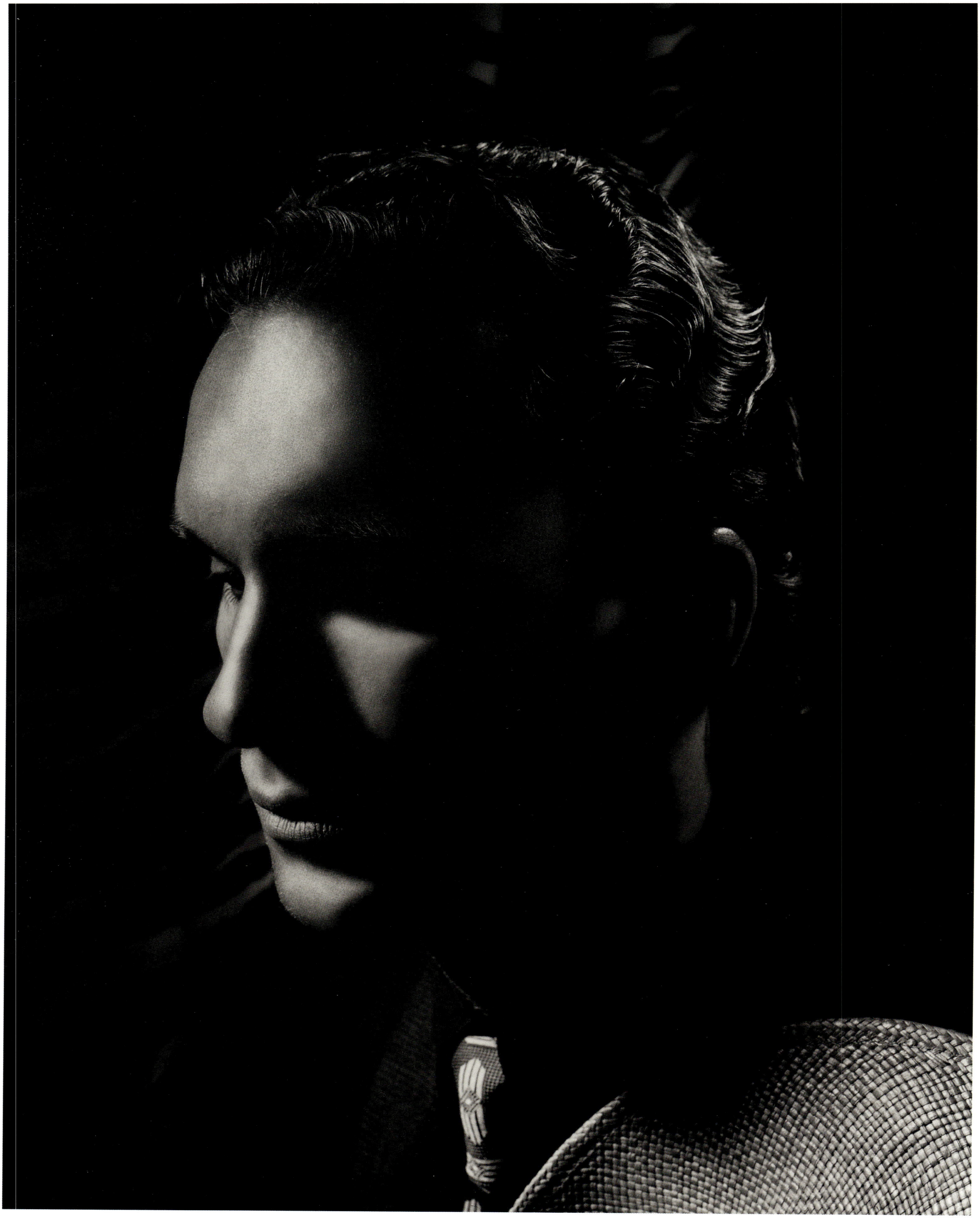

PRECEDING PAGES:

LEFT: JAMES CAVIEZEL, UNION STATION, LOS ANGELES, 1994

RIGHT: DINA MEYER, STUDIO 70/70 C, HOLLYWOOD, 1995

PETER GREEN, CHATEAU MARMONT, HOLLYWOOD, 1994

MATT LEBLANC, STUDIO 70/70 C, HOLLYWOOD, 1995

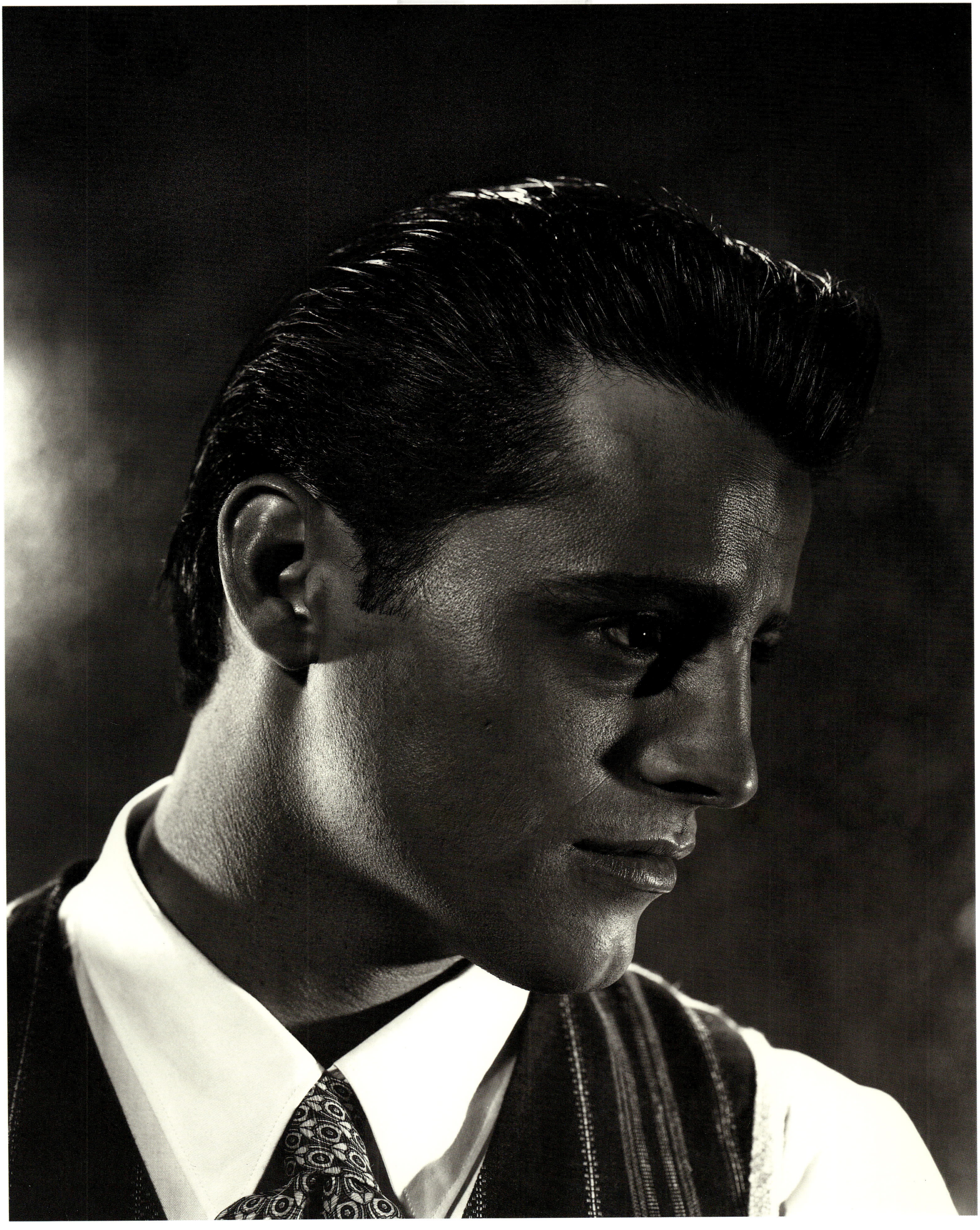

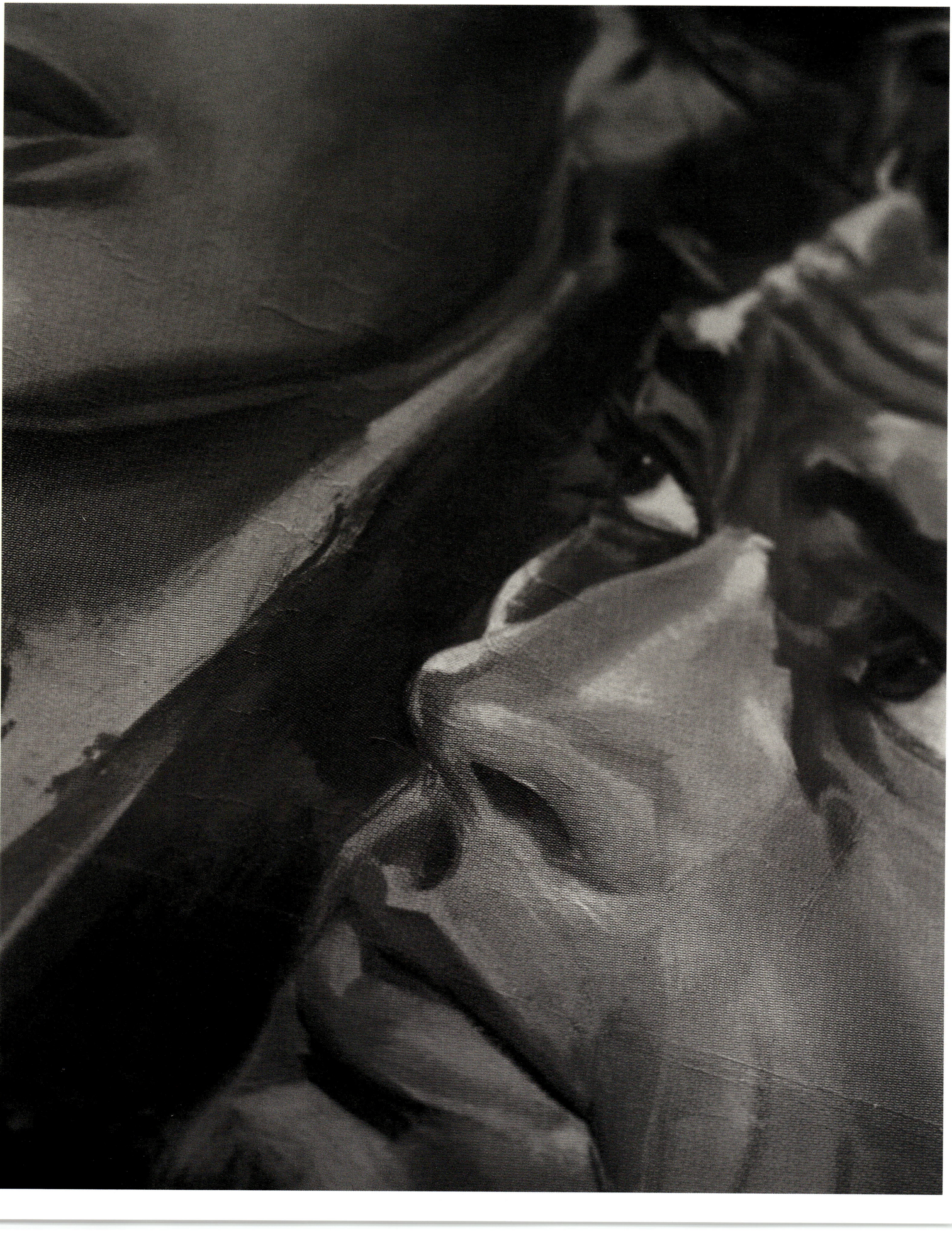

POSTER AT STUDIO 70/70, SANTA MONICA BOULEVARD, 1995

JOHN SHEA, NEW YORK CITY, 1995

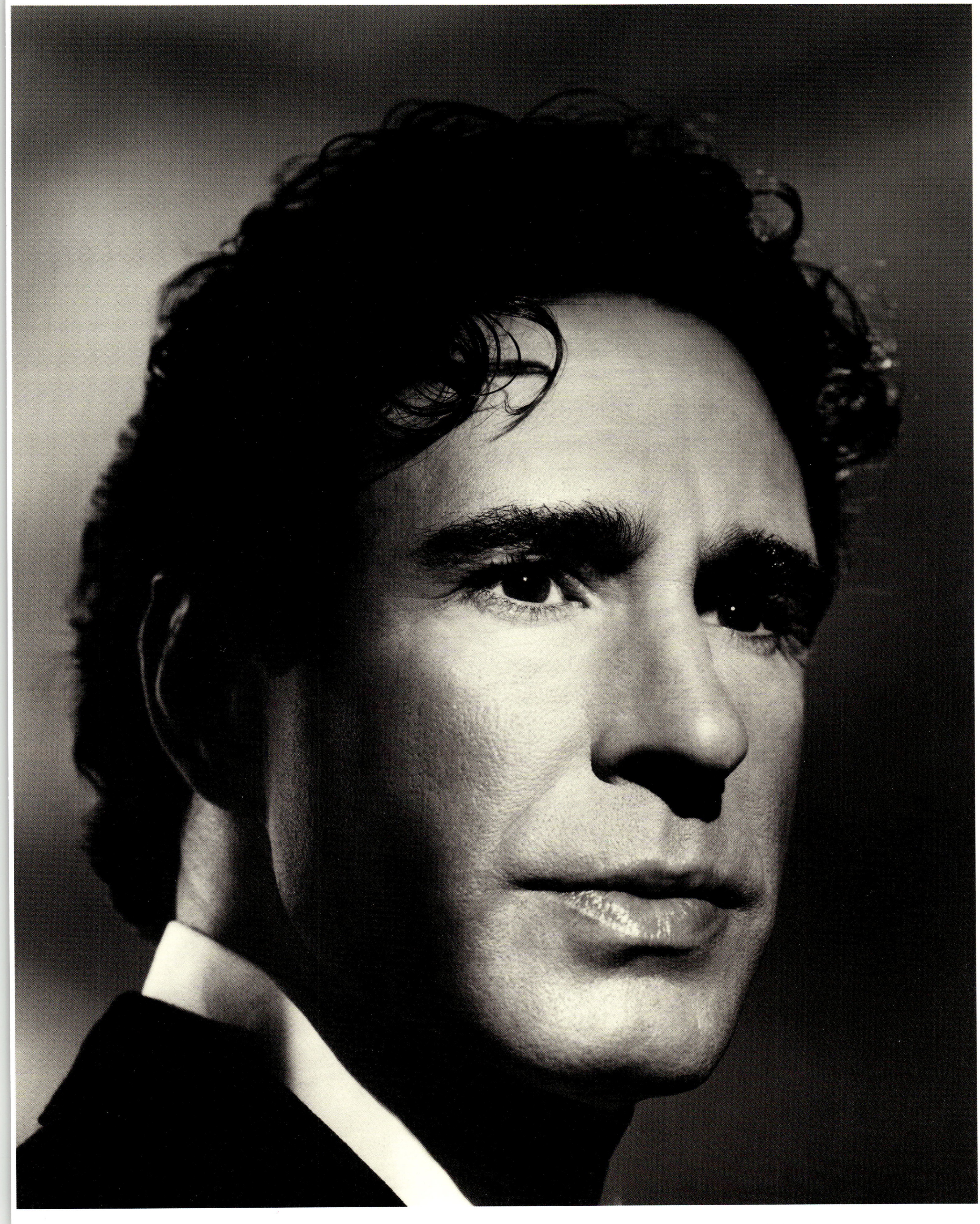

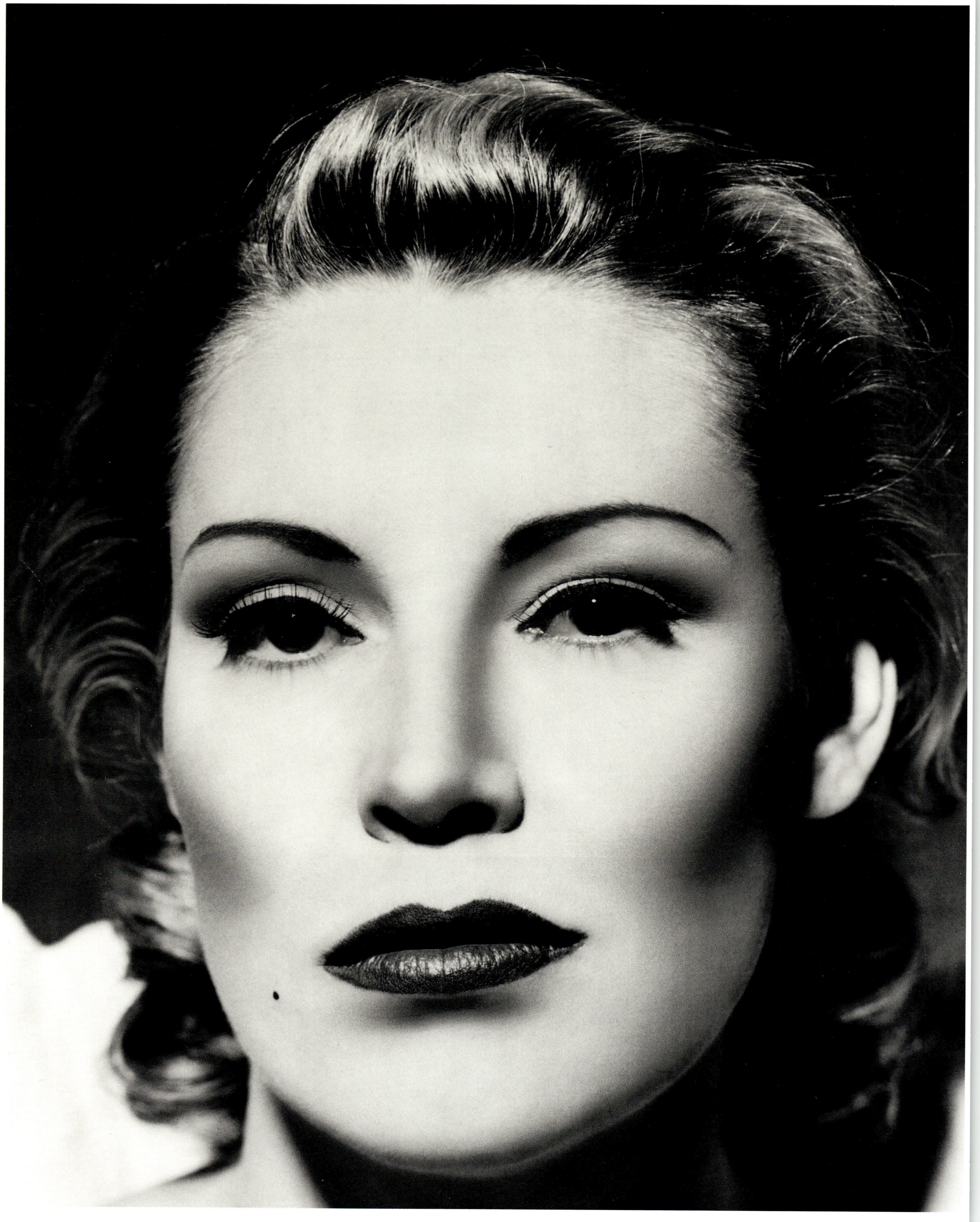

CATHY MORIARTY, STUDIO 70/70 B, SANTA MONICA BOULEVARD, 1994

PETER WELLER, HOLLYWOOD, 1994

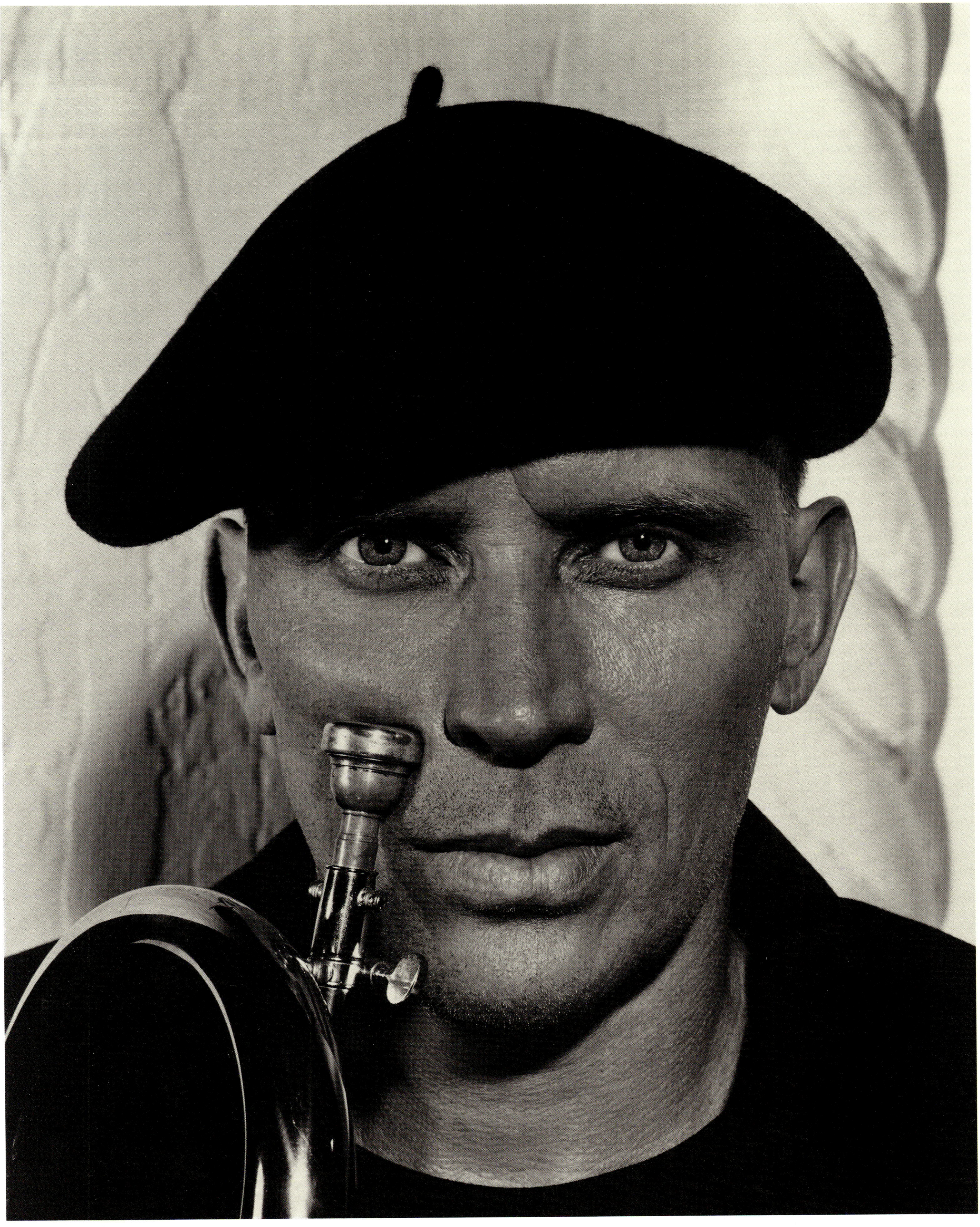

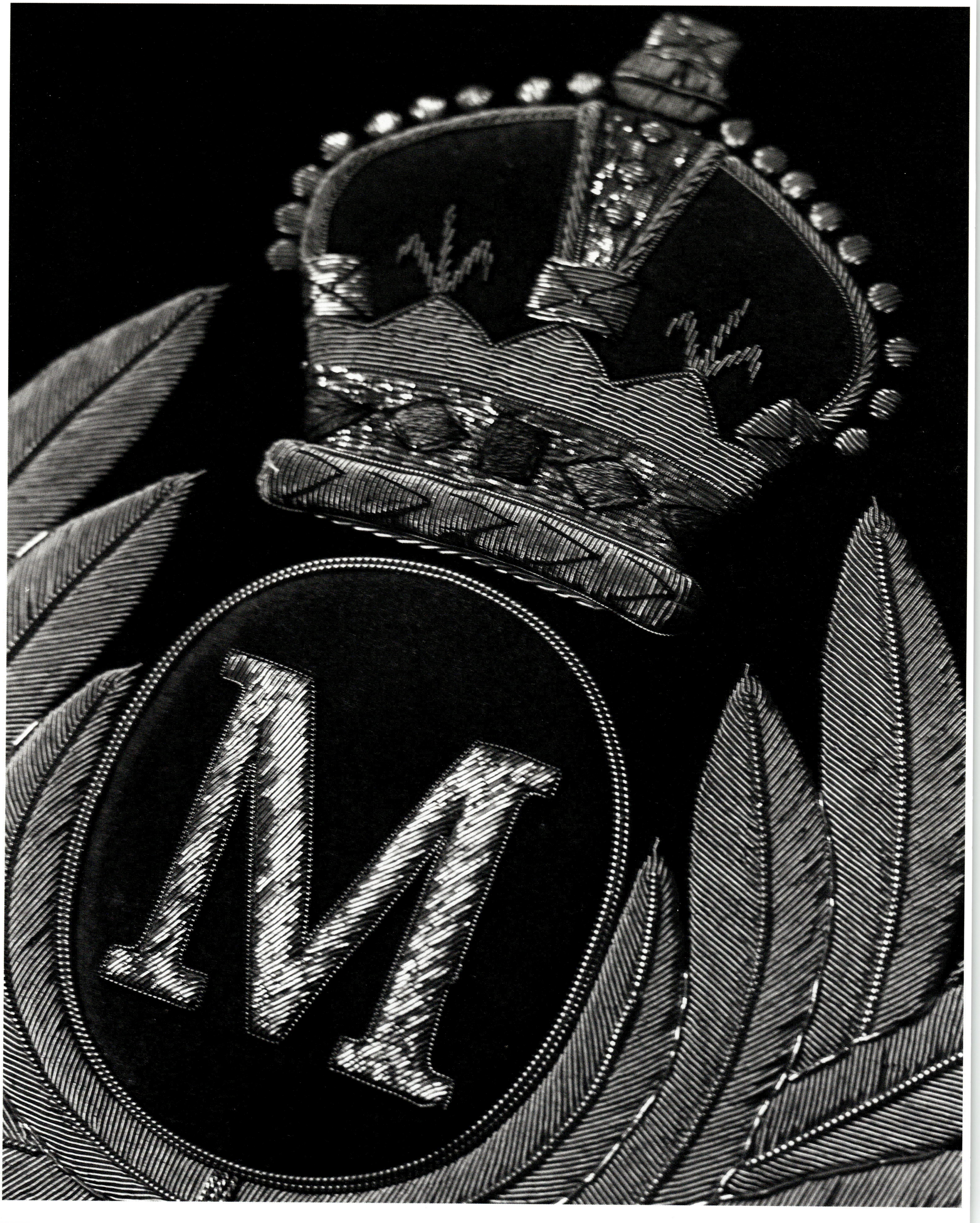

MANCUSO CREST, MANCUSO ESTATE, BEVERLY HILLS, 1995

MAUREEN ORTH, CARLYLE HOTEL, WASHINGTON, D.C., 1996

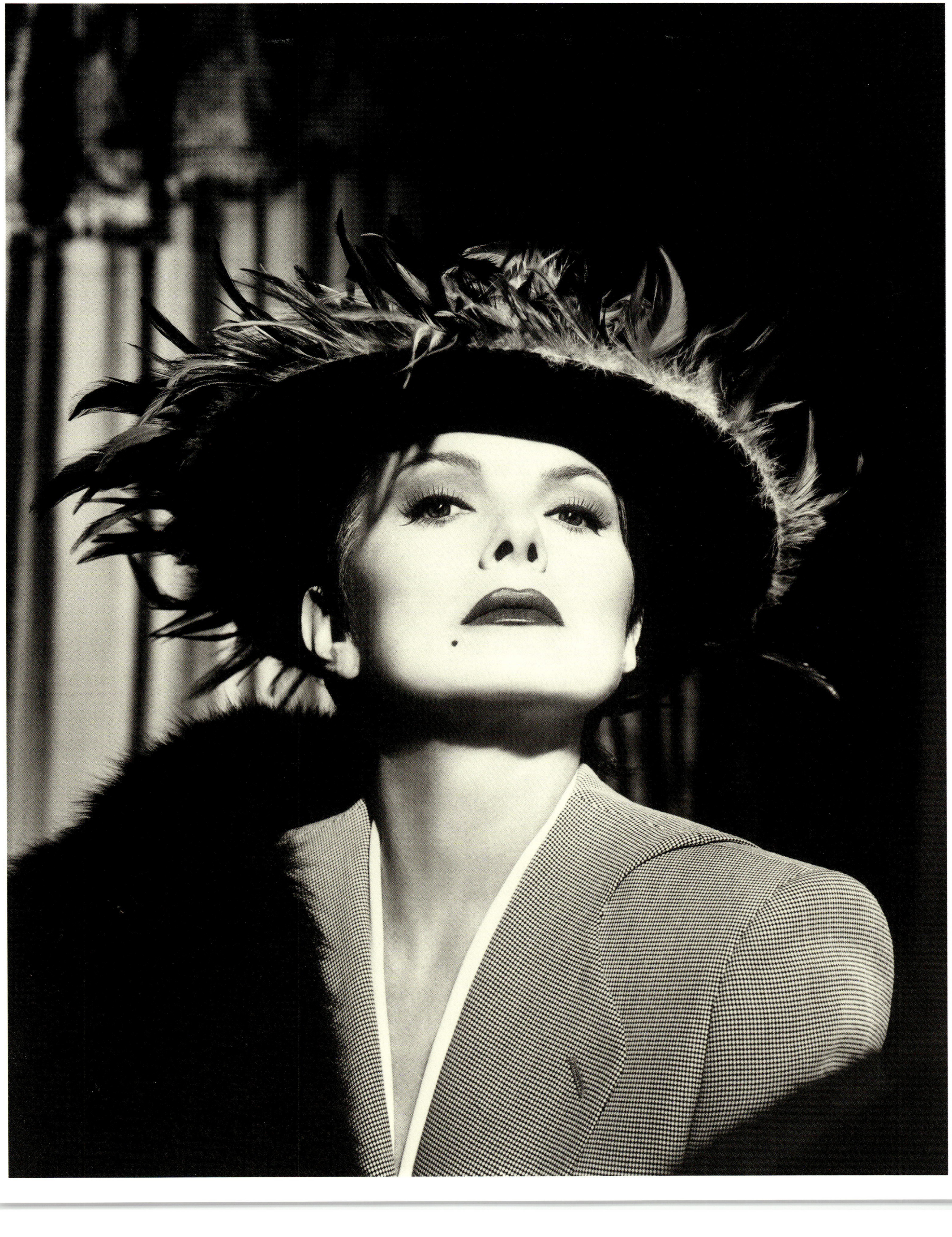

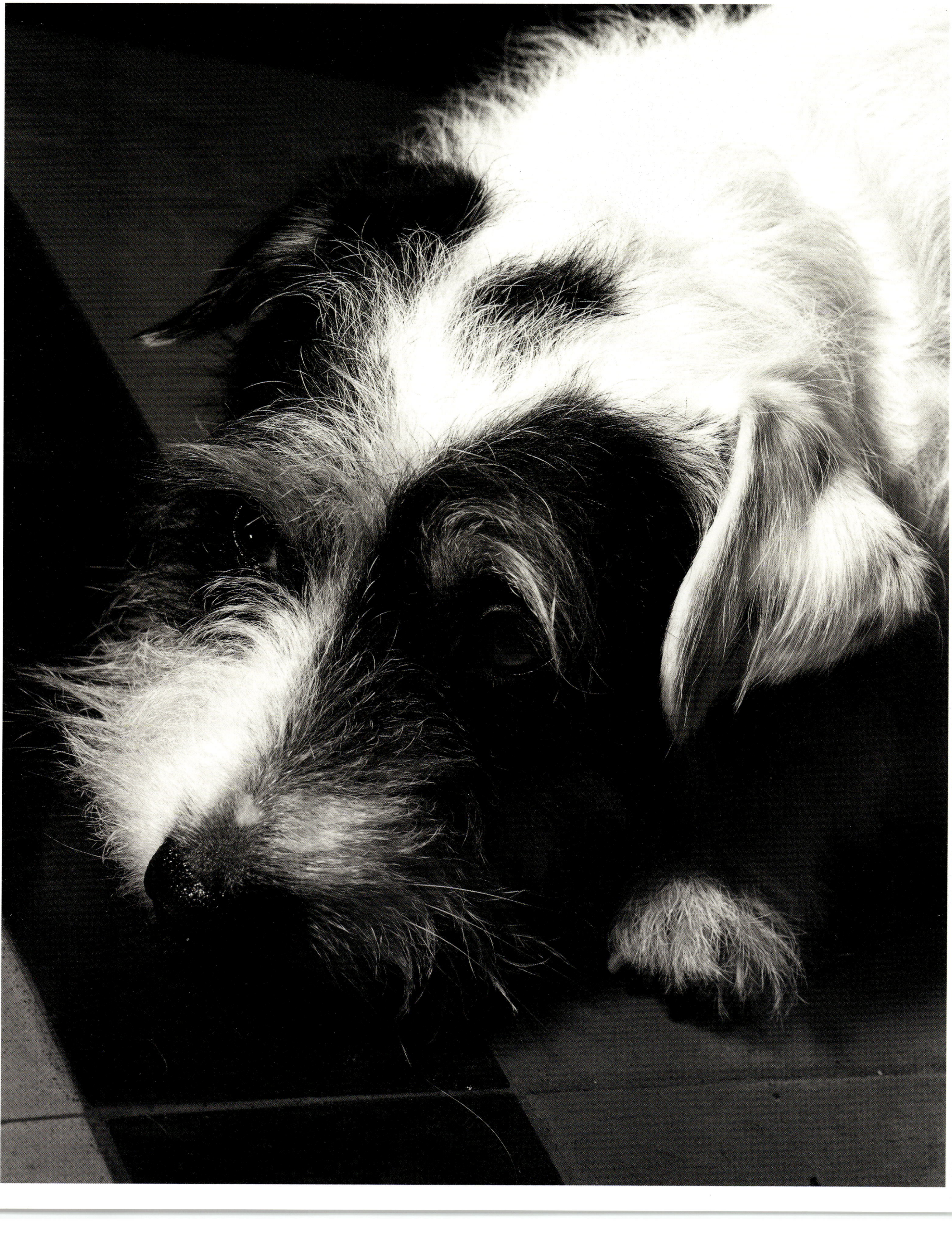

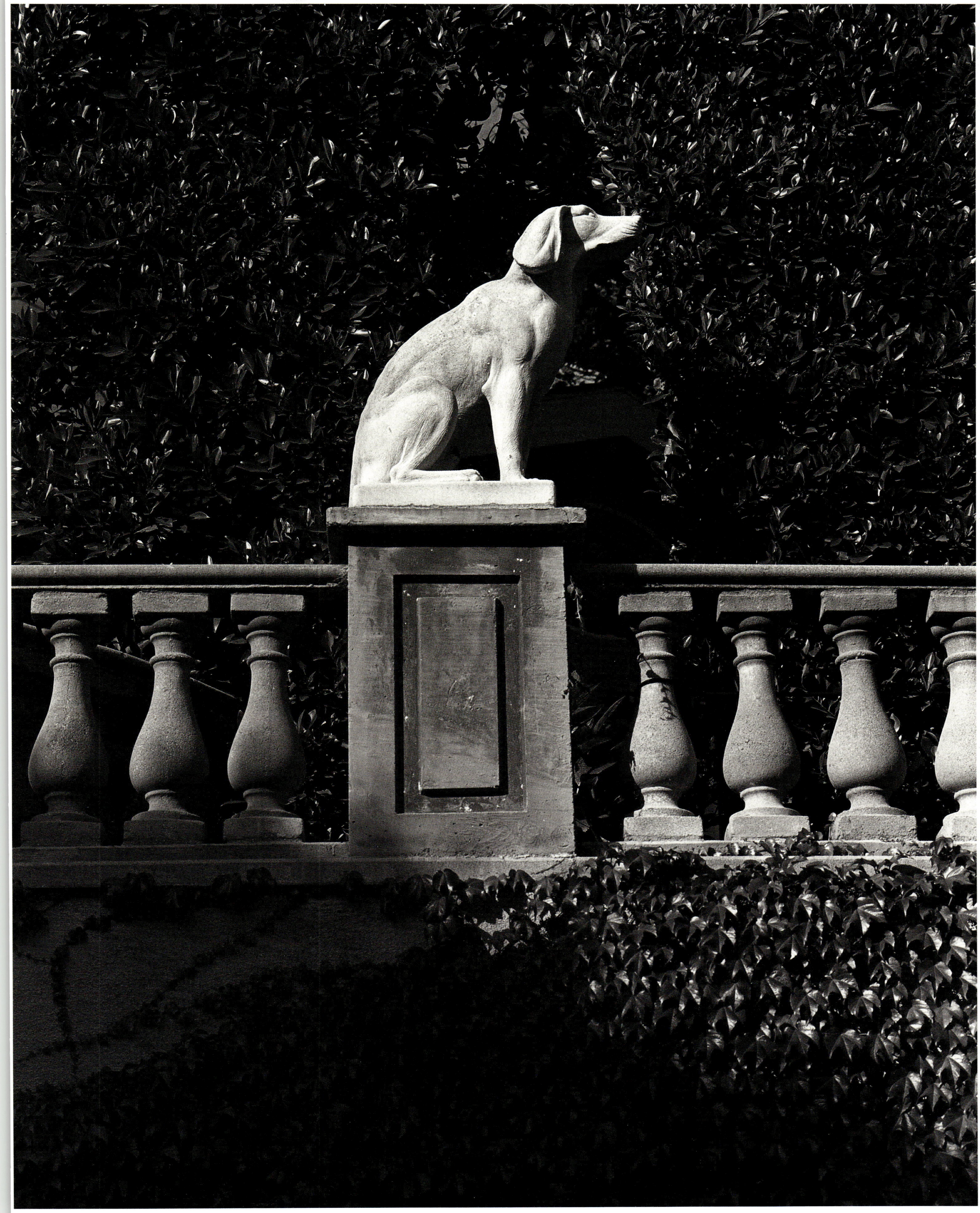

PRECEDING PAGES:

LEFT: RUPERT, UNION STATION, LOS ANGELES, 1994

RIGHT: CEMENT DOG, HOLLYWOOD, 1996

JULIE NEWMAR, BRENTWOOD, 1994

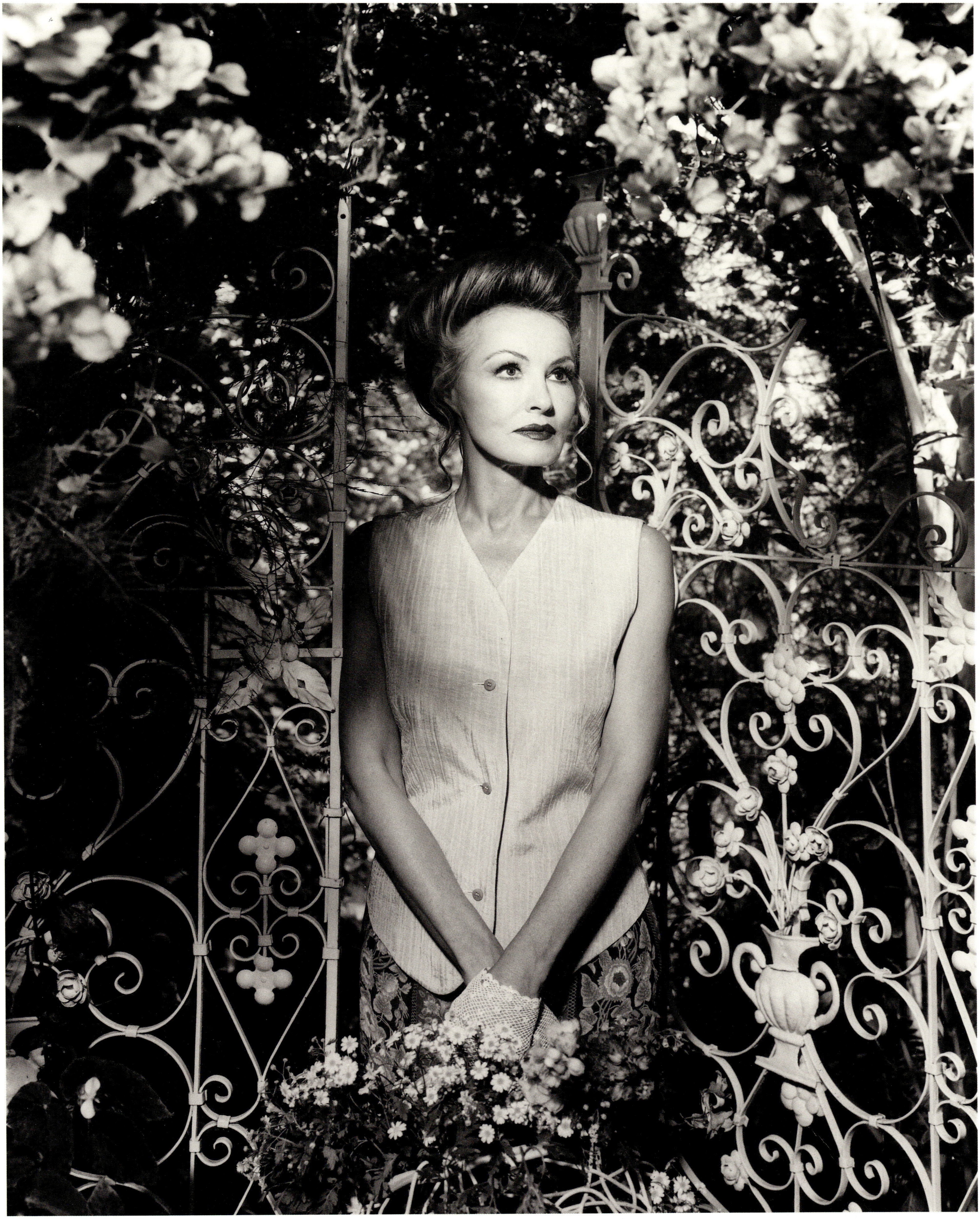

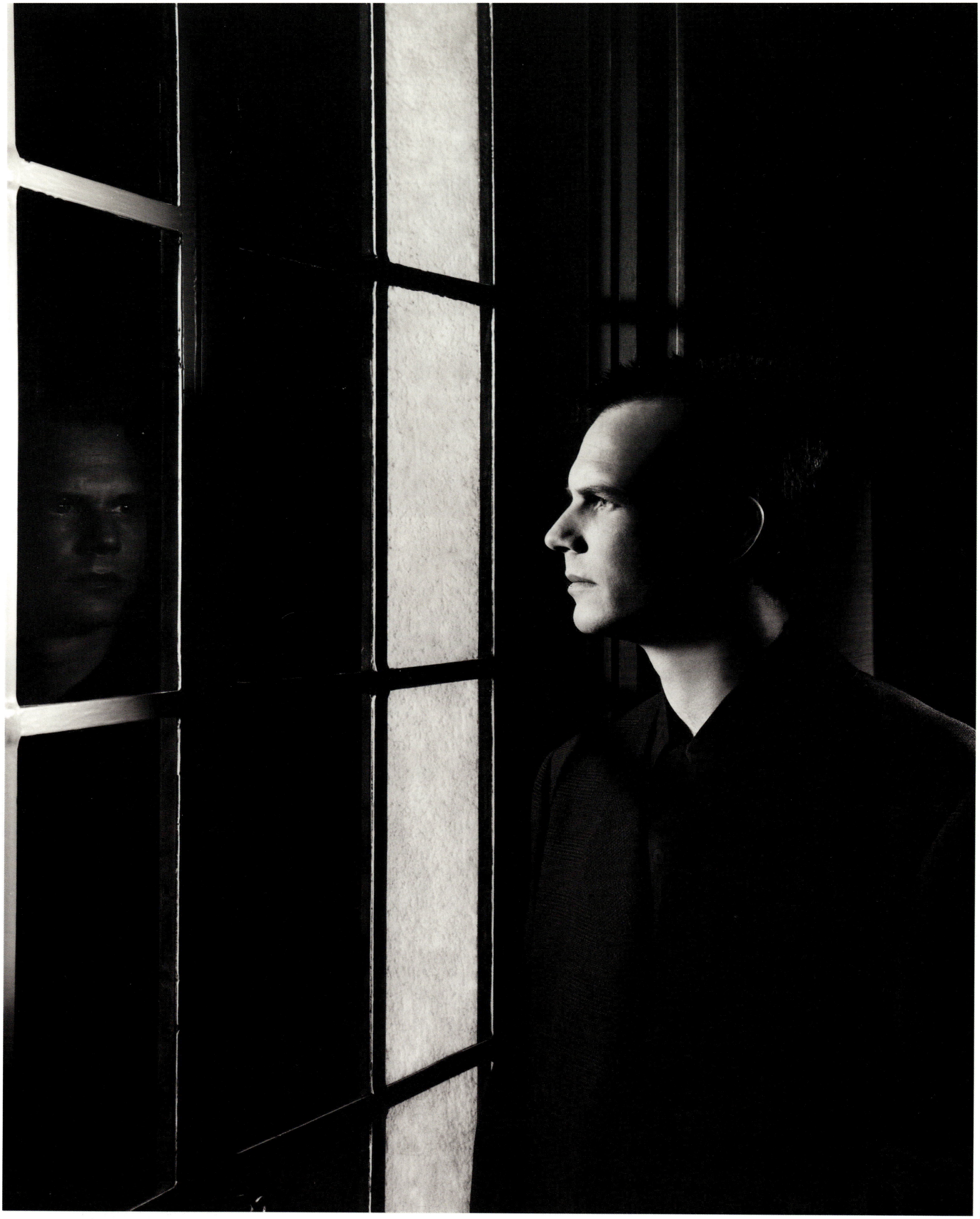

BILL PAXTON, CHATEAU MARMONT, HOLLYWOOD, 1994

AIDAN QUINN, CHATEAU MARMONT, HOLLYWOOD, 1994

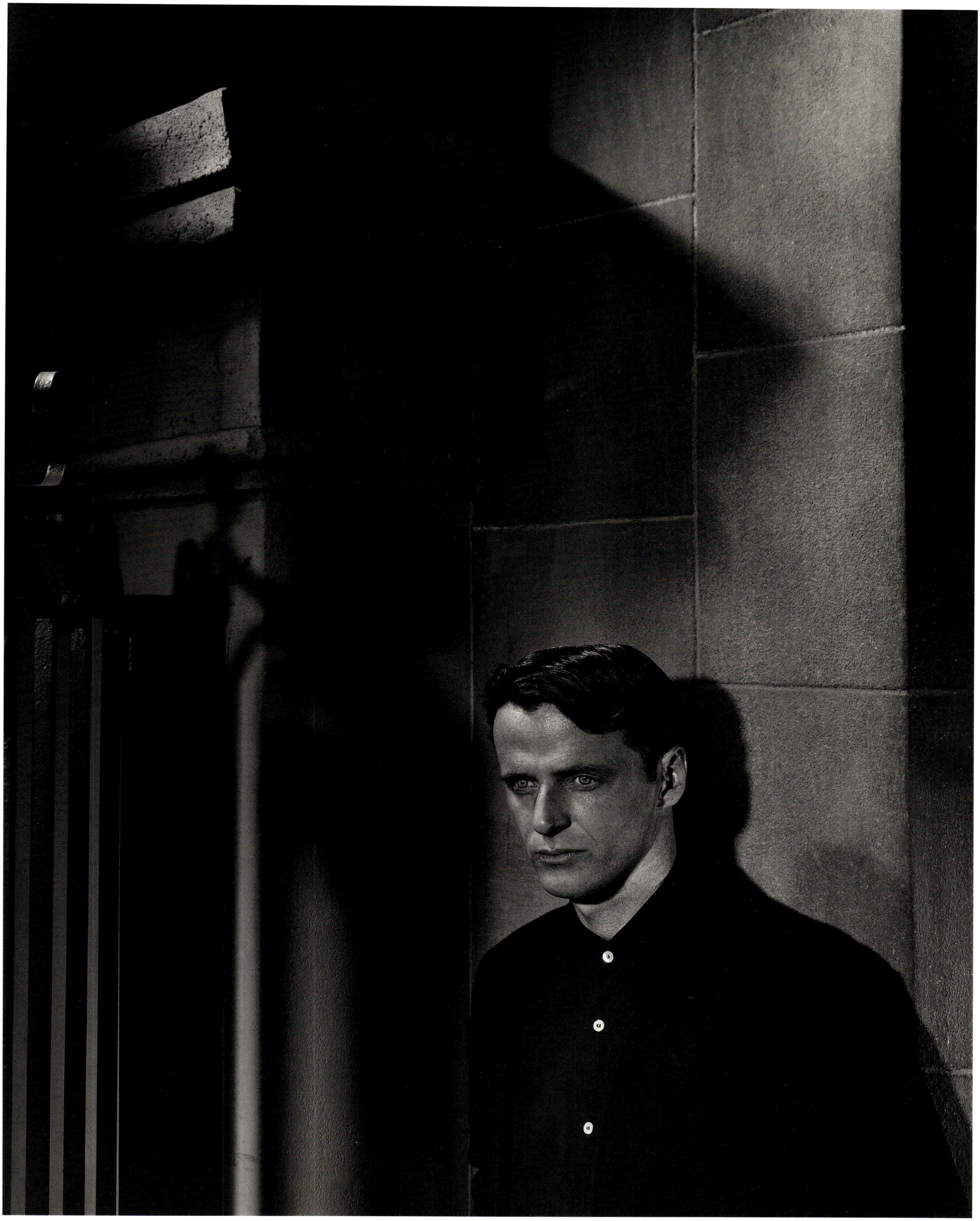

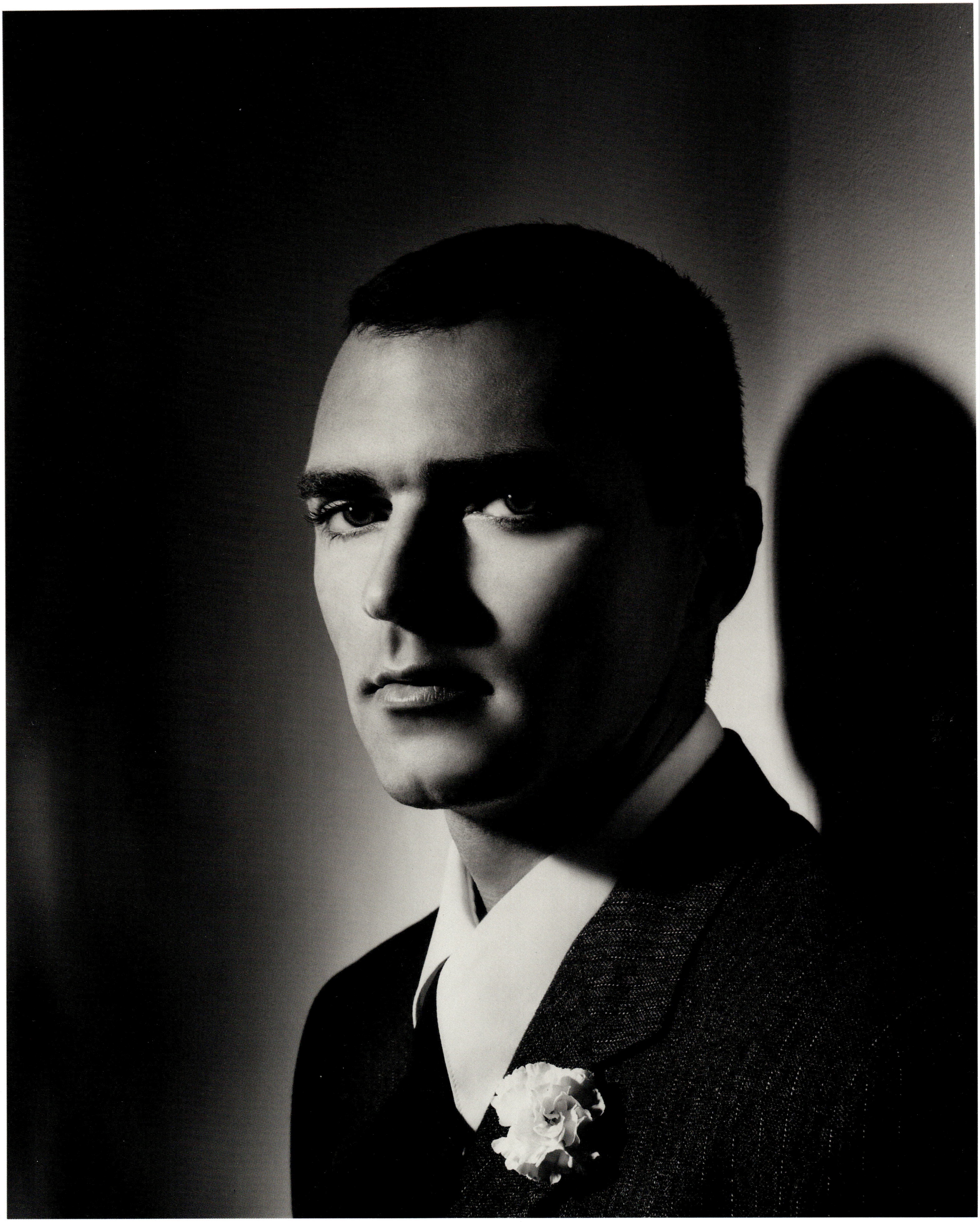

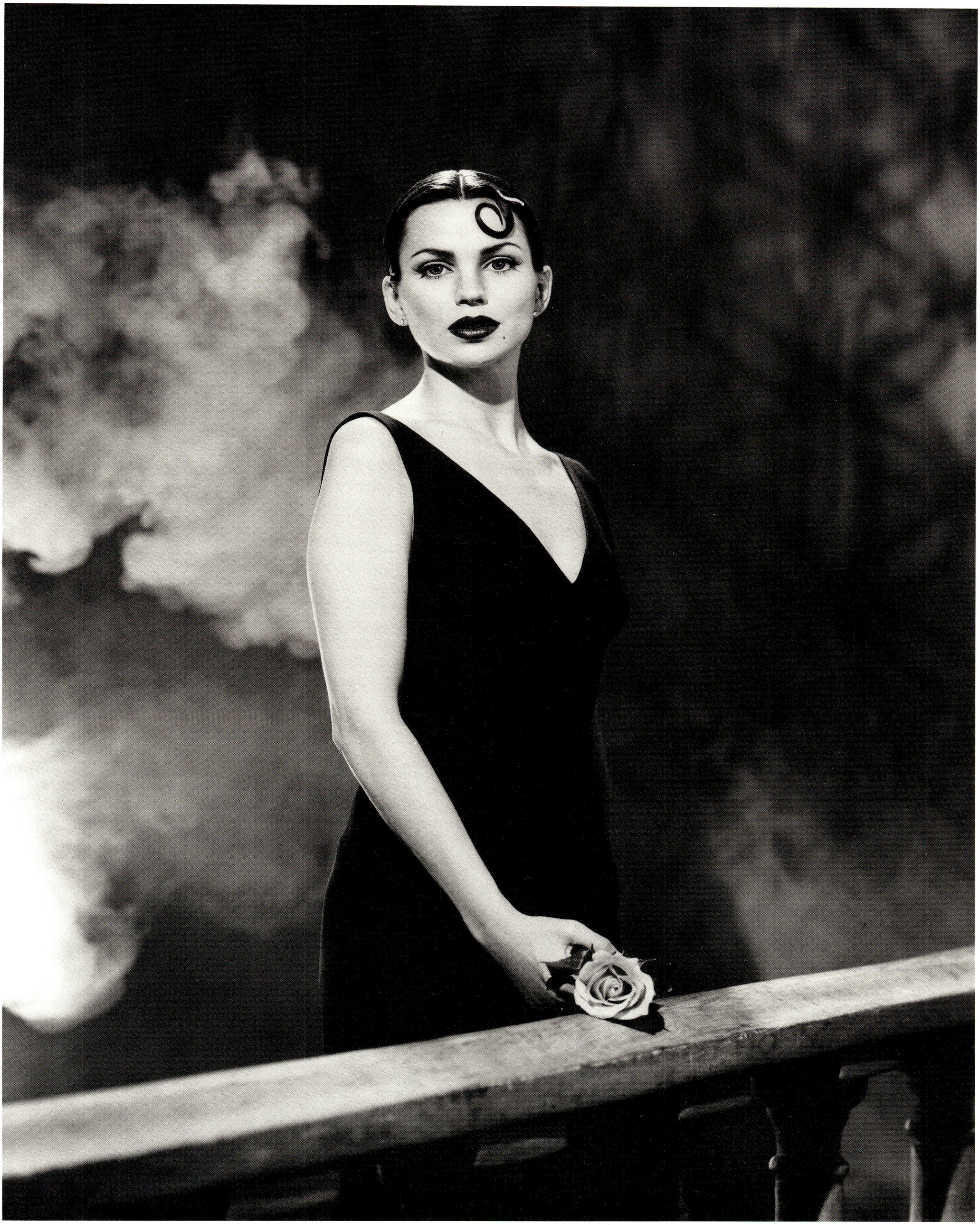

PRECEDING PAGES:

LEFT: CHRISTOPHER CICCONE, NEW YORK CITY, 1994

RIGHT: KAREN DUFFY, NEW YORK CITY, 1994

ISABELLE HUPPERT, NEW YORK CITY, 1994

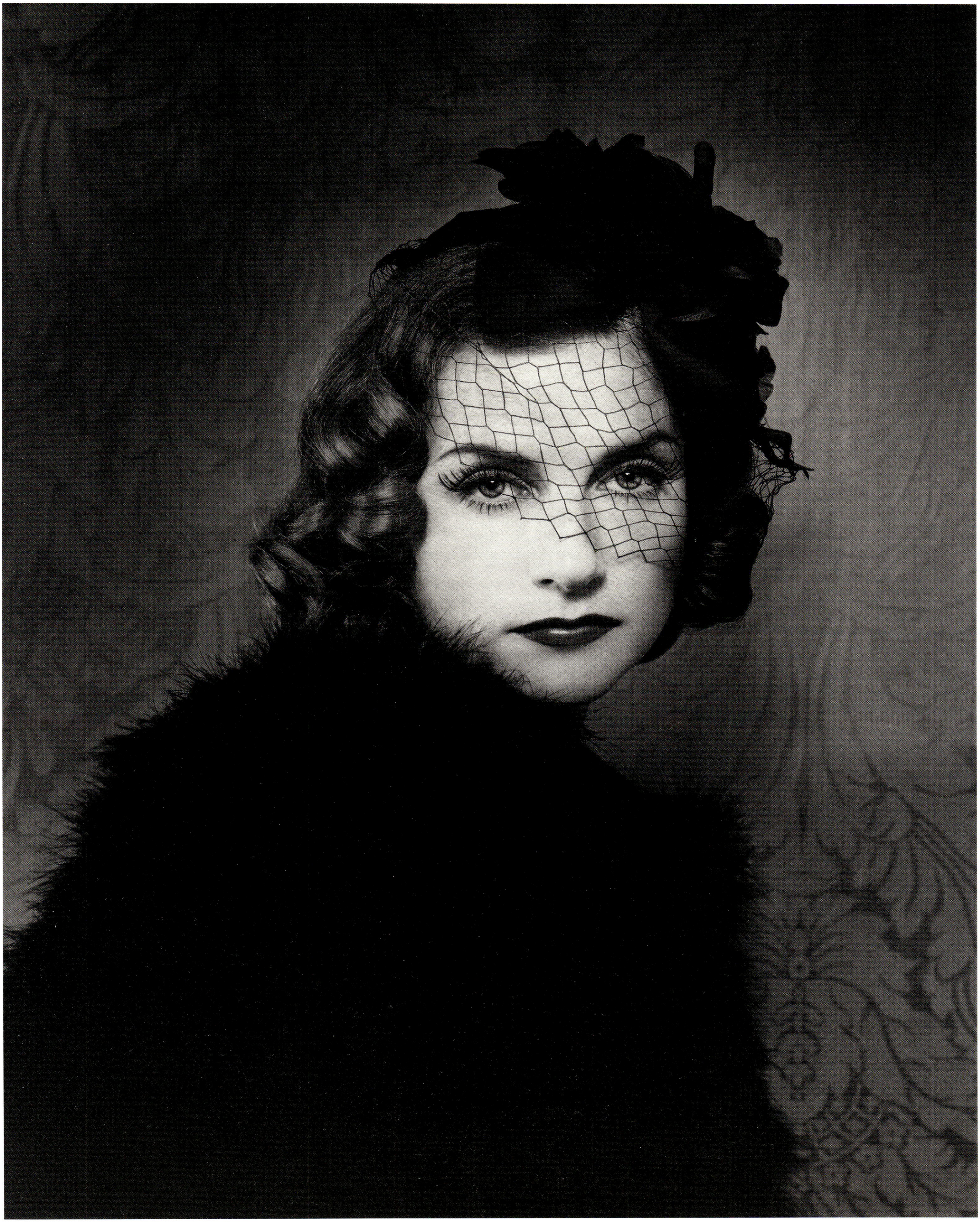

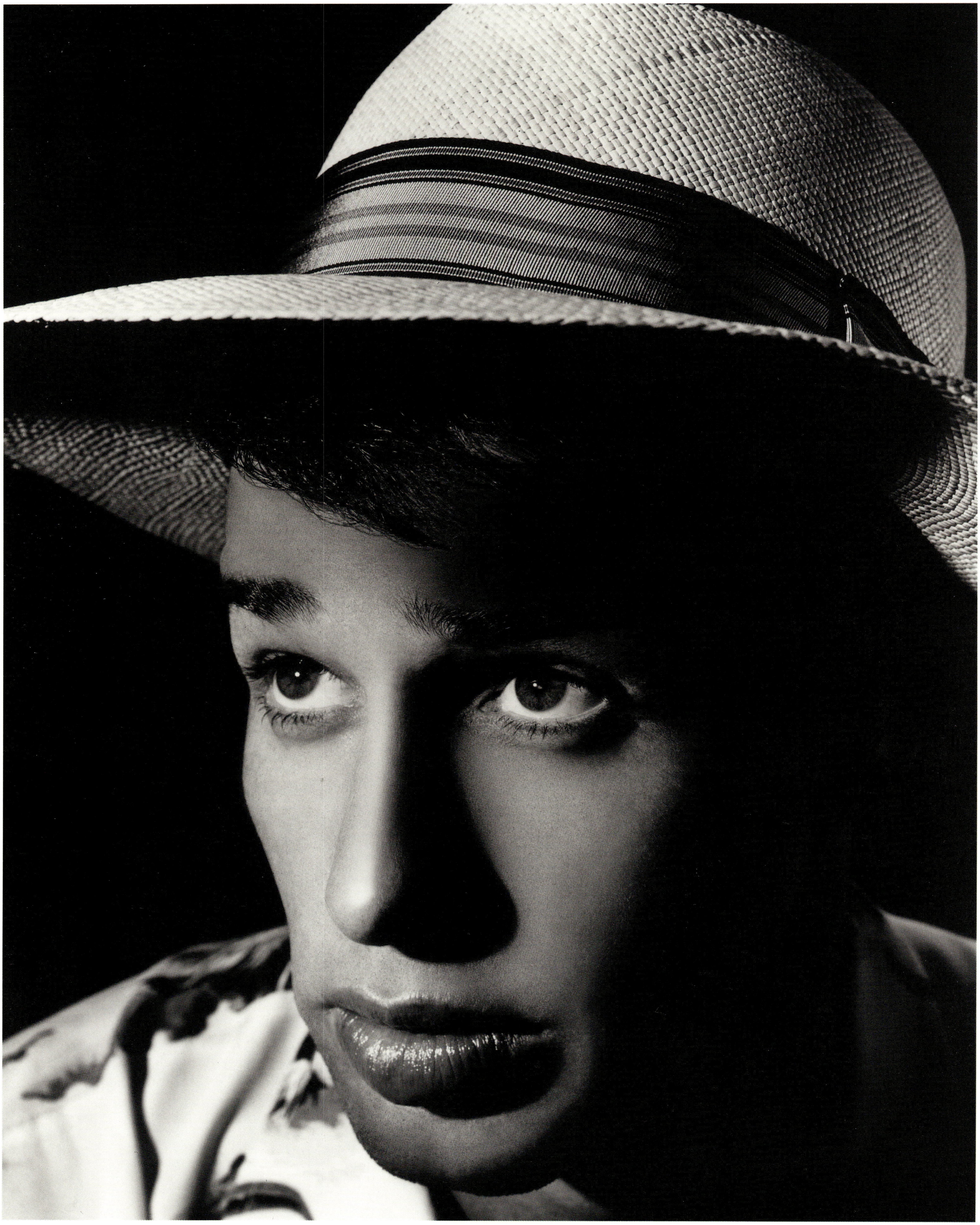

ALEXIS ARQUETTE, CHATEAU MARMONT, HOLLYWOOD, 1994

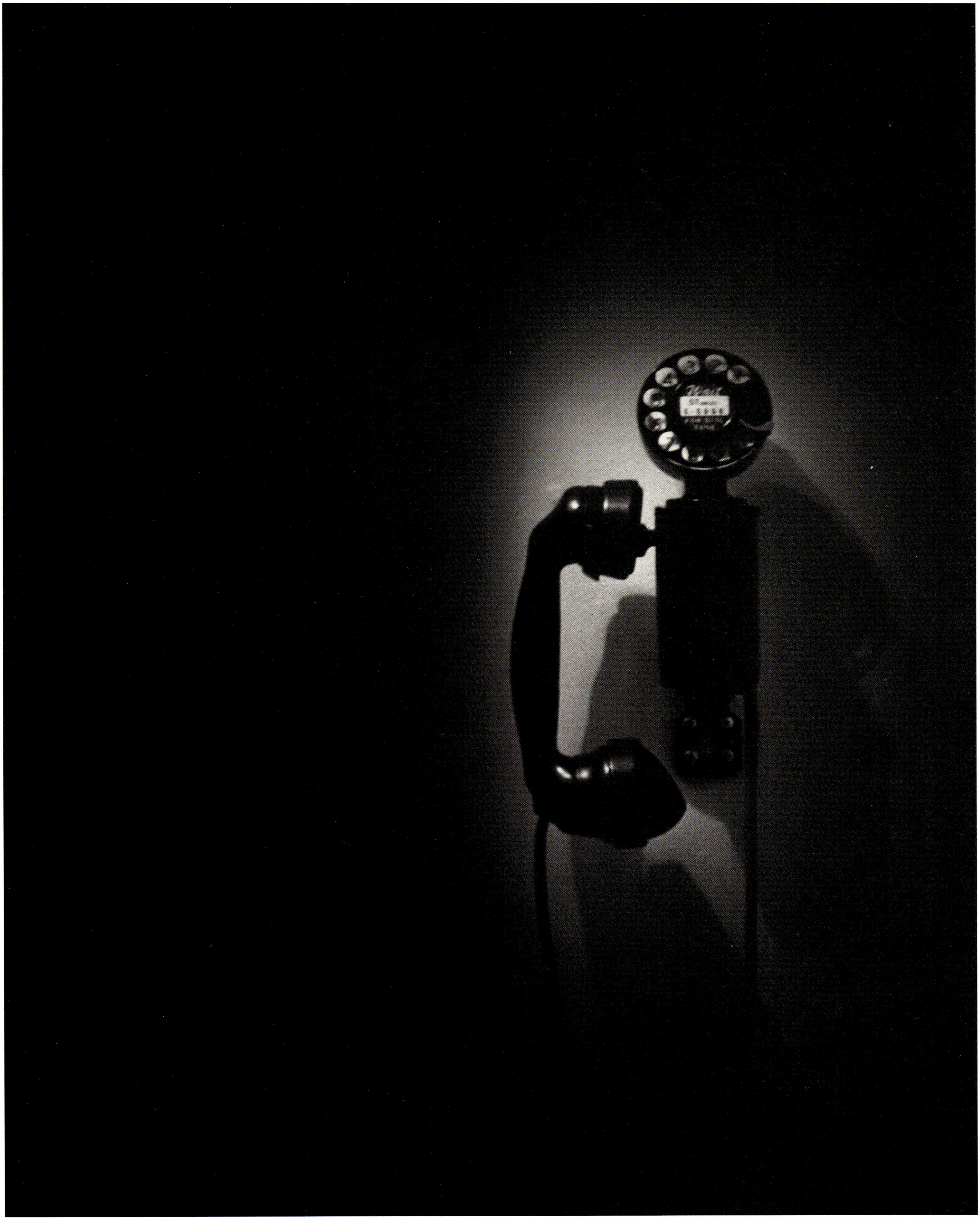

PRECEDING PAGES:

LEFT: SELF-PORTRAIT, CHATEAU MARMONT, HOLLYWOOD, 1996

RIGHT: HOUSE TELEPHONE, CHATEAU MARMONT, HOLLYWOOD, 1994

KIM MANCUSO, BEVERLY HILLS, 1994

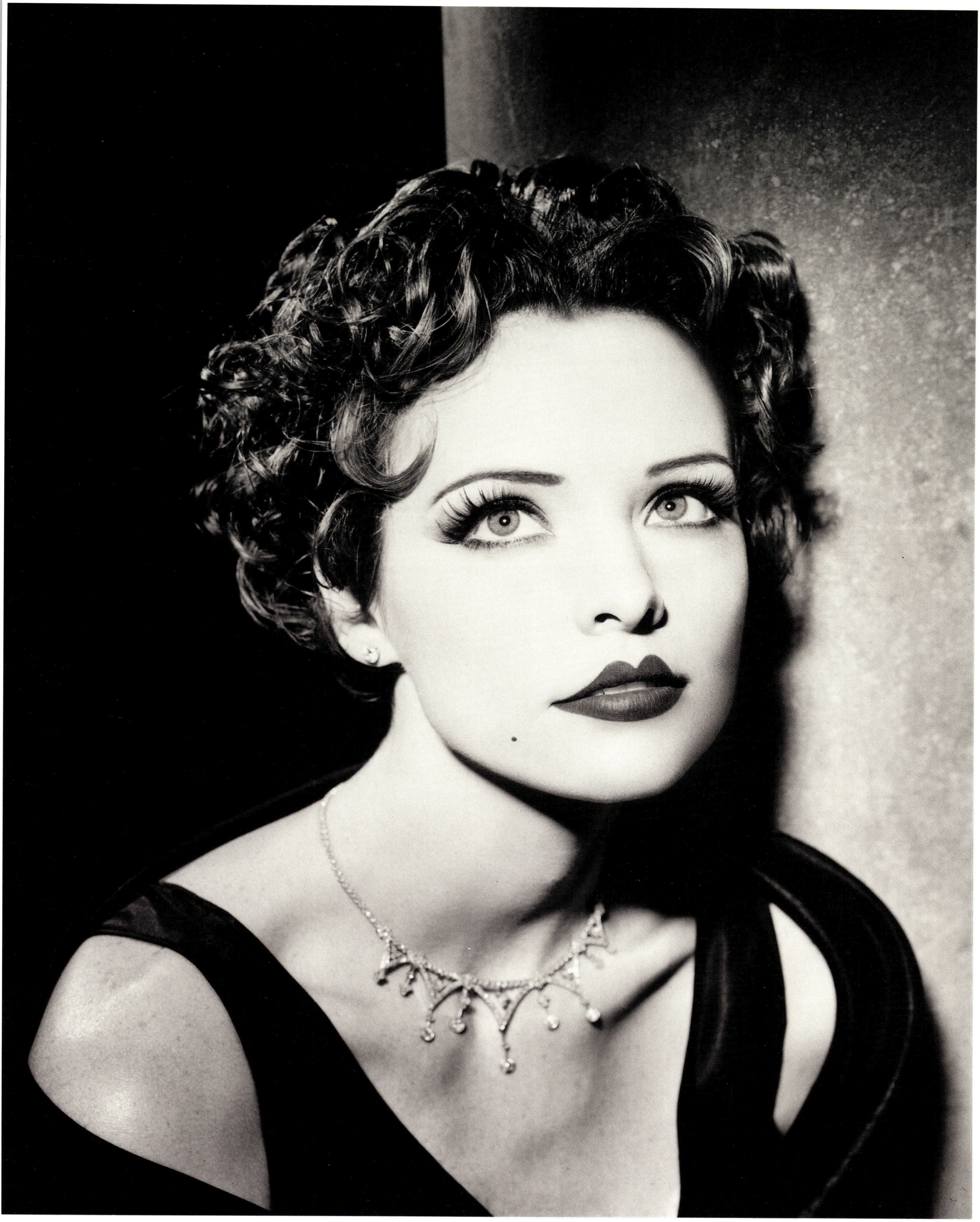

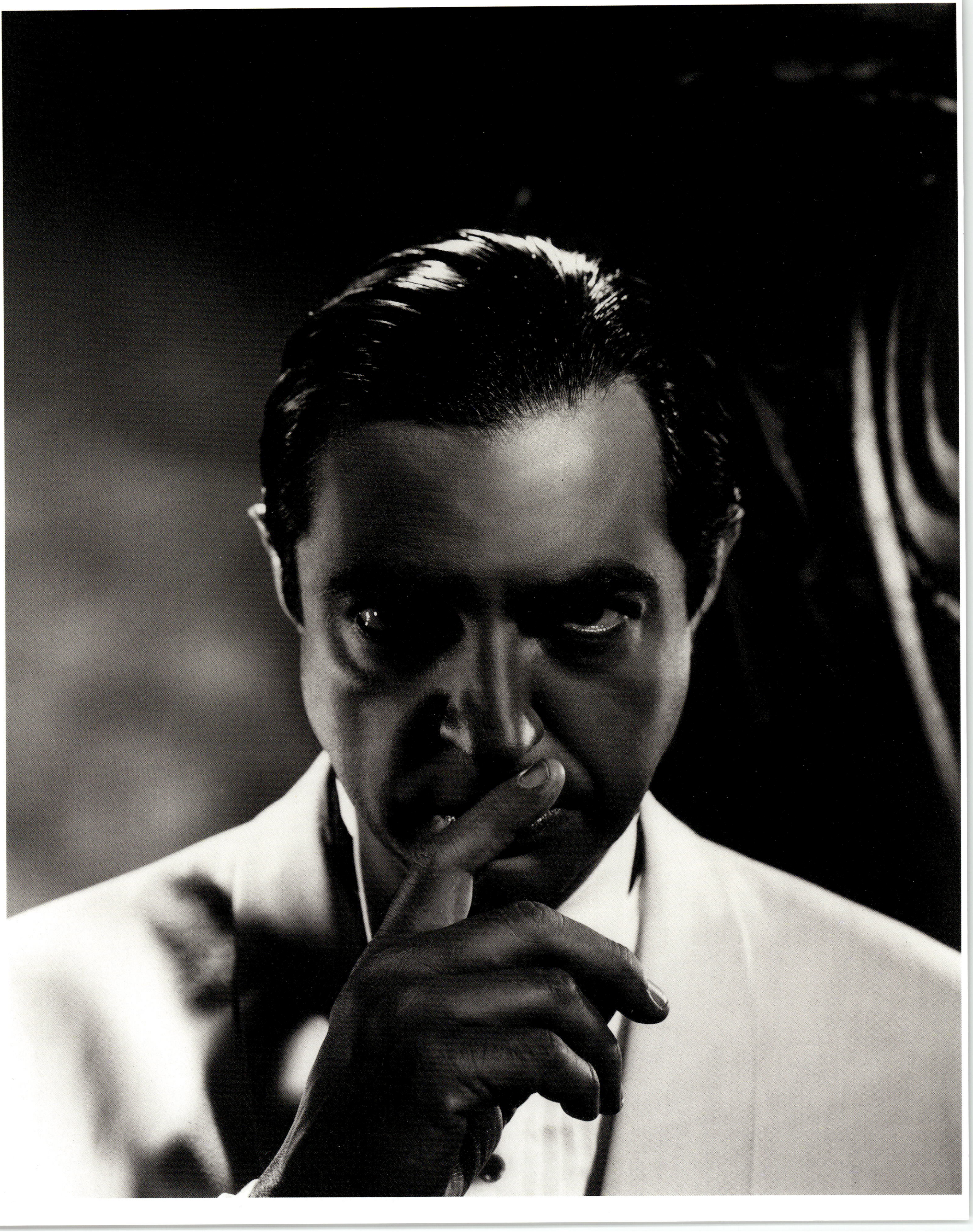

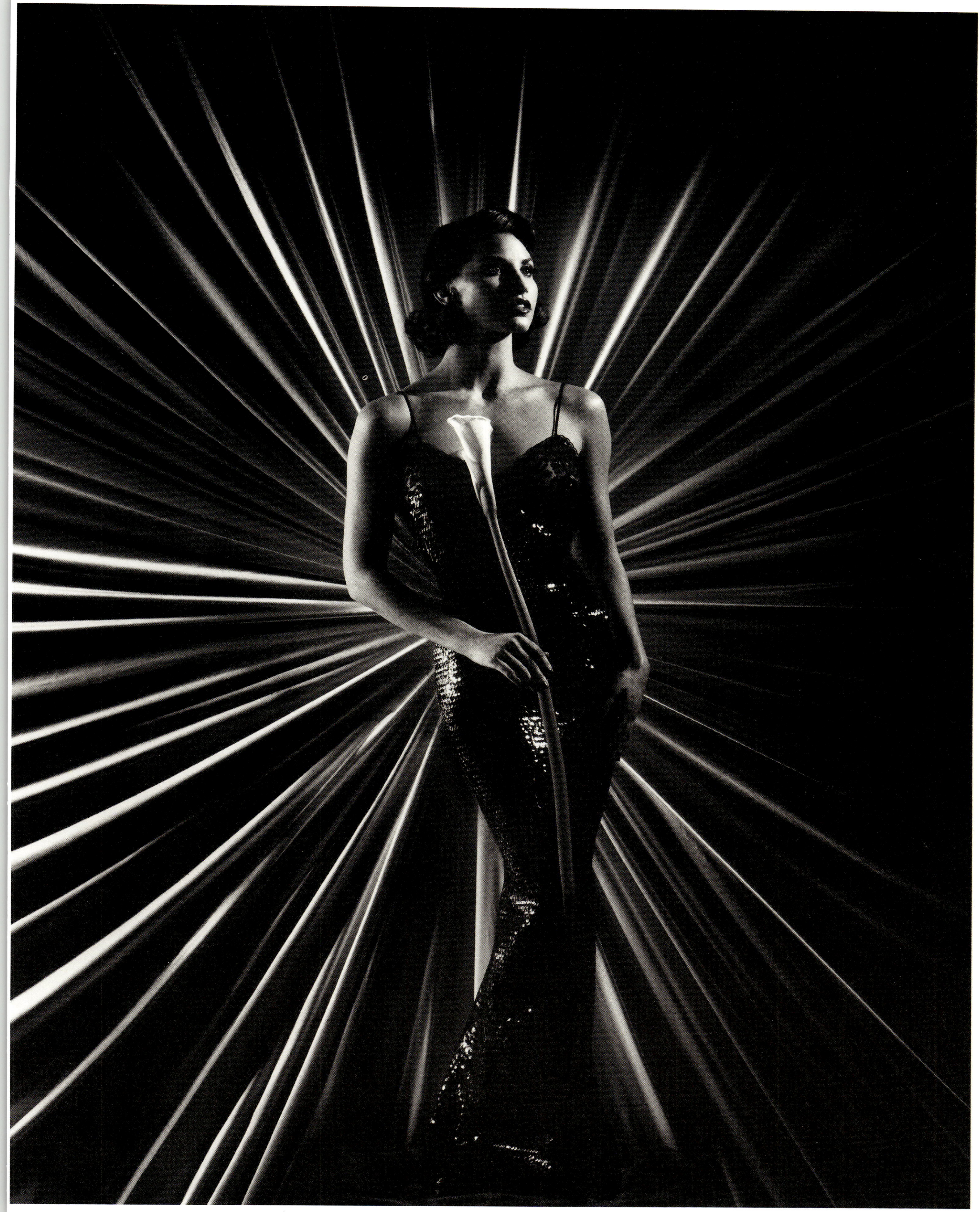

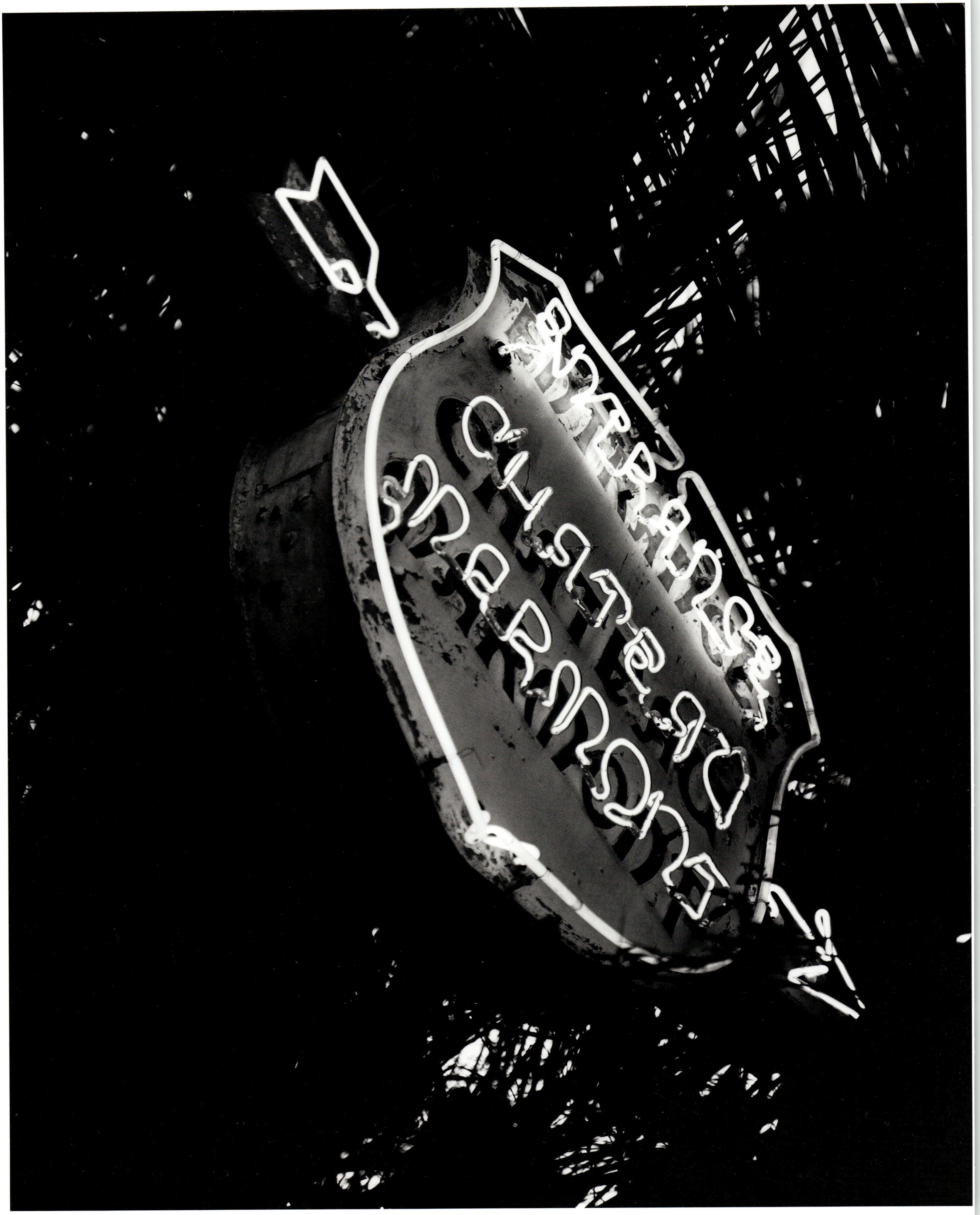

PRECEDING PAGES:

LEFT: JOE MANTEGNA, STUDIO 70/70 C, HOLLYWOOD, 1995

RIGHT: GINA GERSHON, NEW YORK CITY, 1996

CHATEAU MARMONT, HOLLYWOOD, 1994

JEREMY JORDAN, CHATEAU MARMONT, HOLLYWOOD, 1994

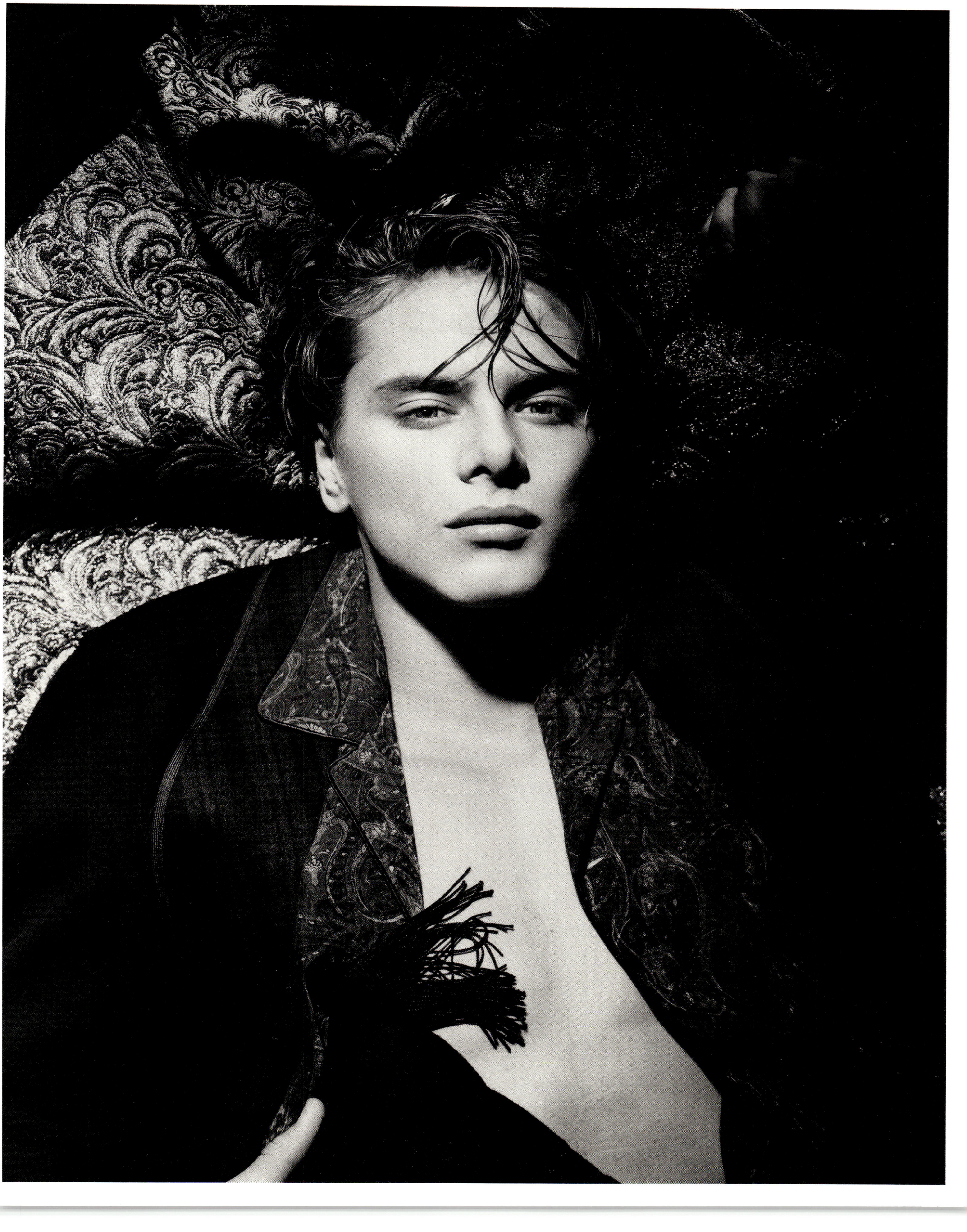

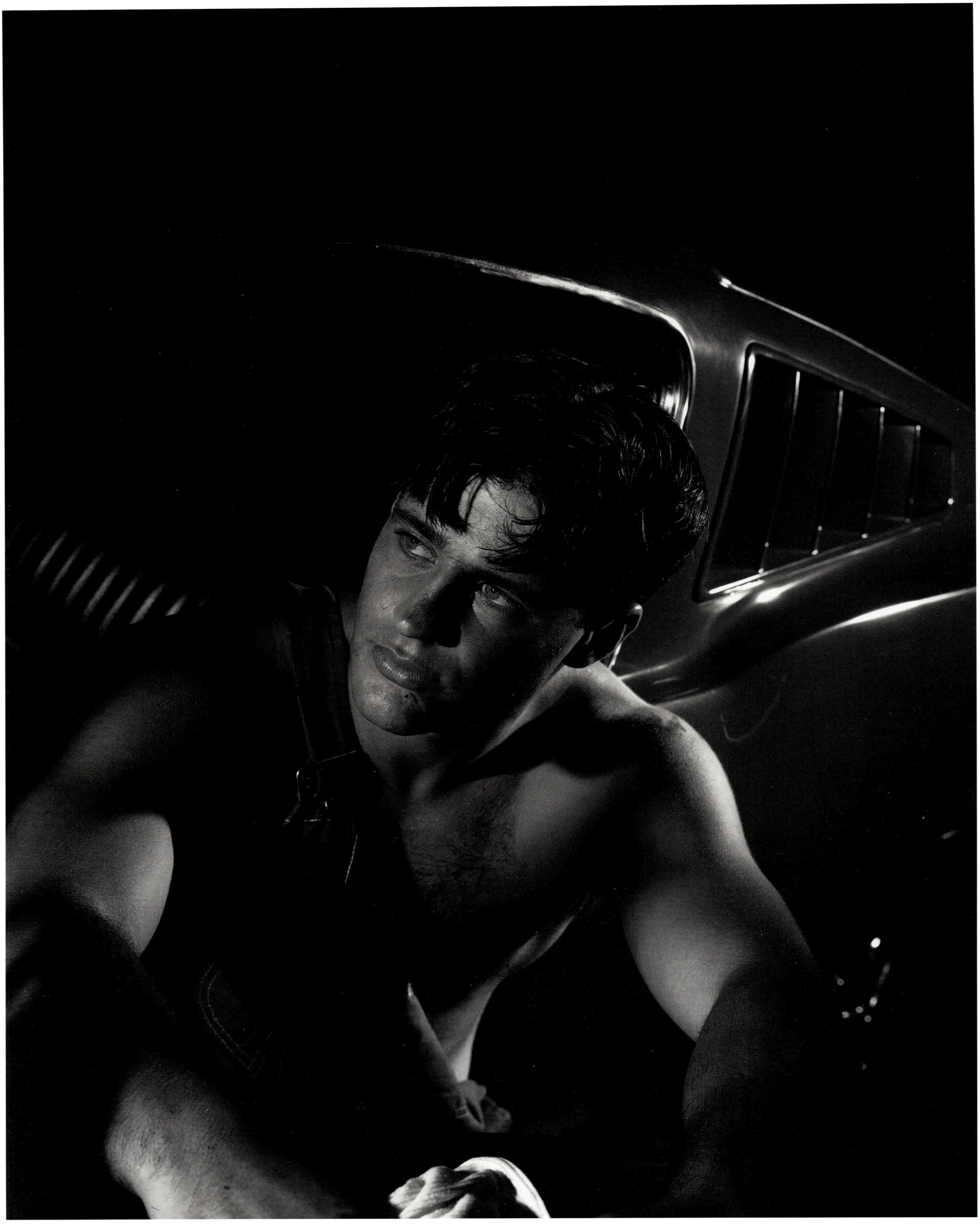

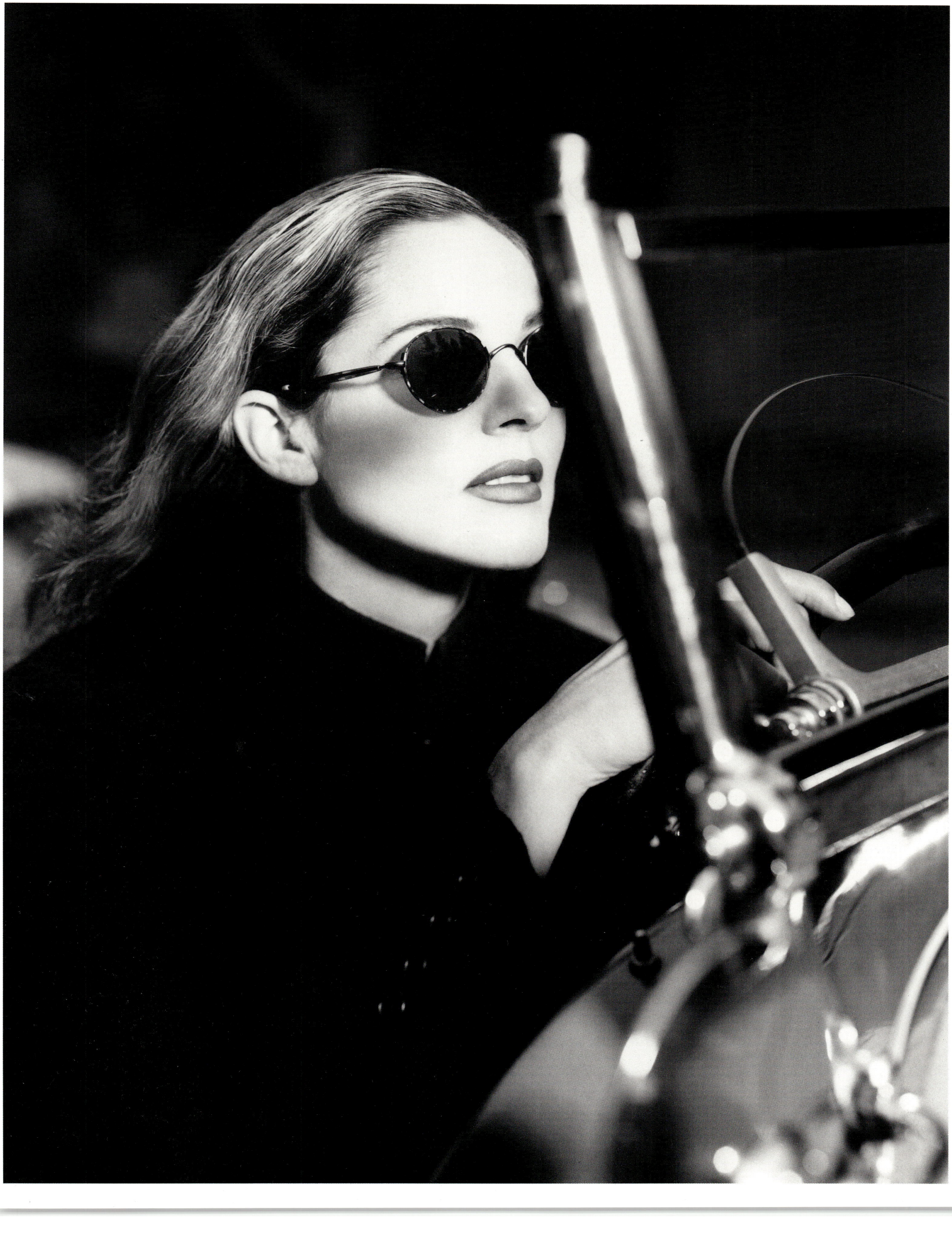

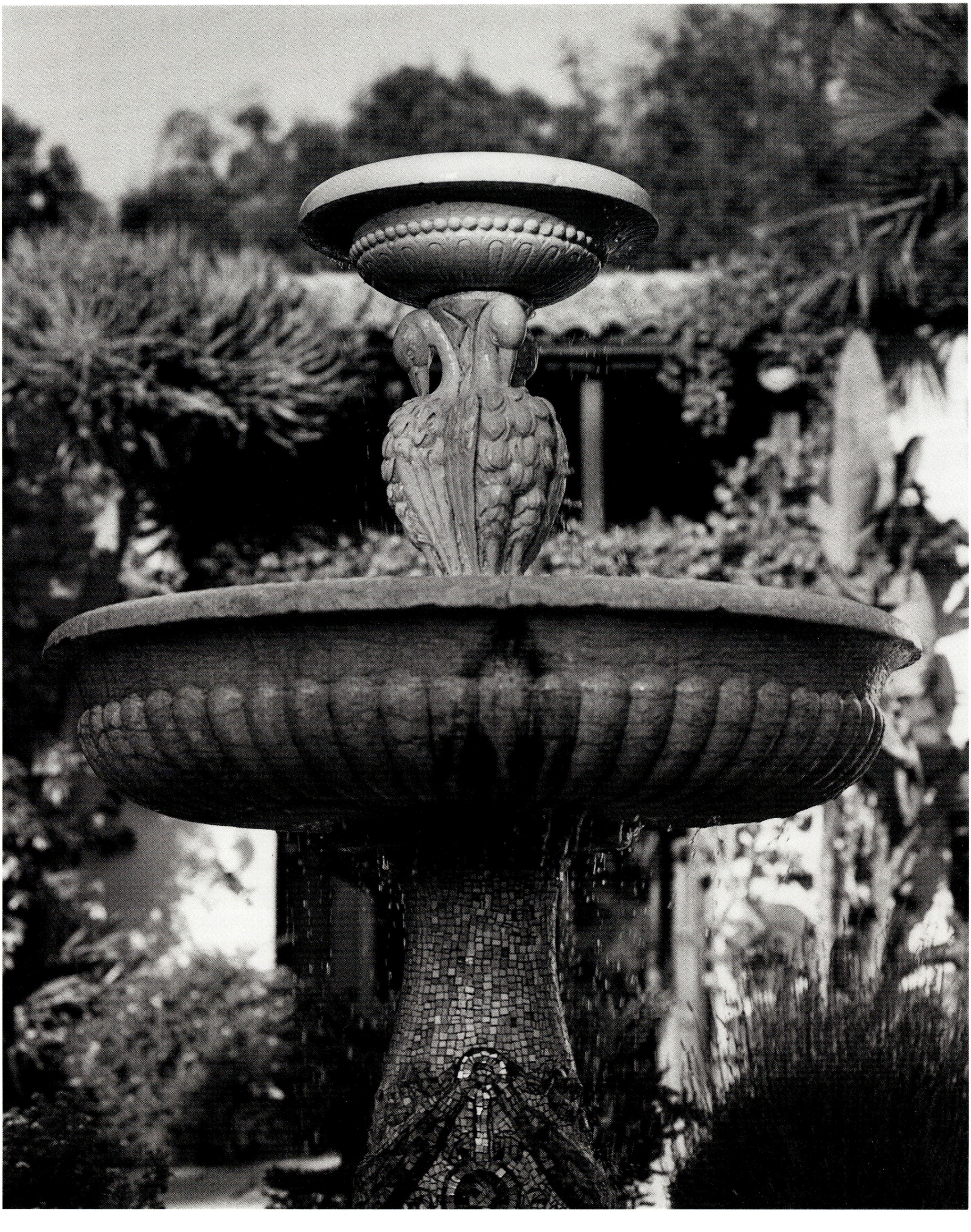

PRECEDING PAGES:

LEFT: LOUIS MANDYLOR, CHATEAU MARMONT, HOLLYWOOD, 1994

RIGHT: KELLY KLEIN, BEVERLY HILLS, 1994

FOUNTAIN, MANCUSO ESTATE, BEVERLY HILLS, 1994

SELA WARD, STUDIO 70/70 C. HOLLYWOOD, 1995

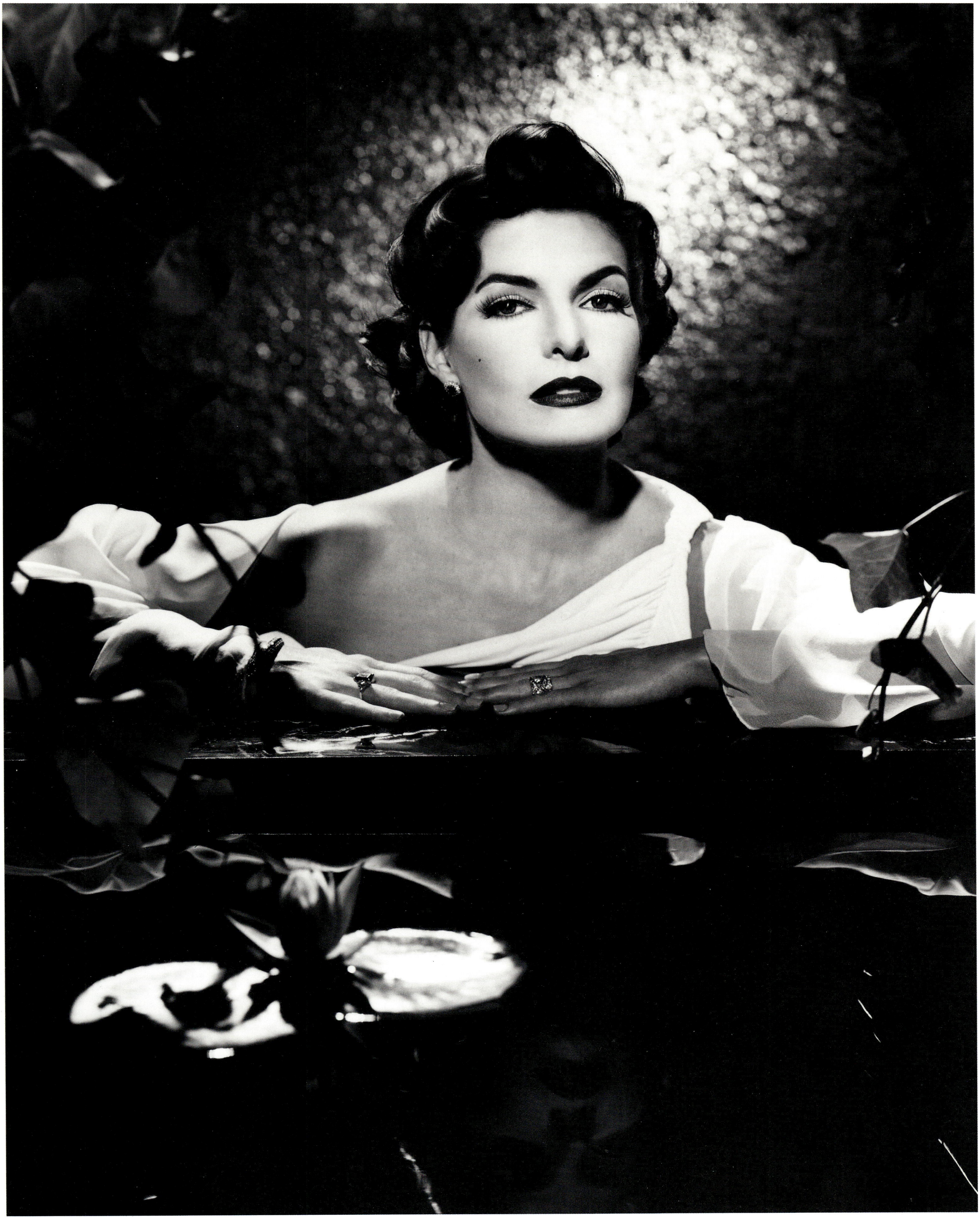

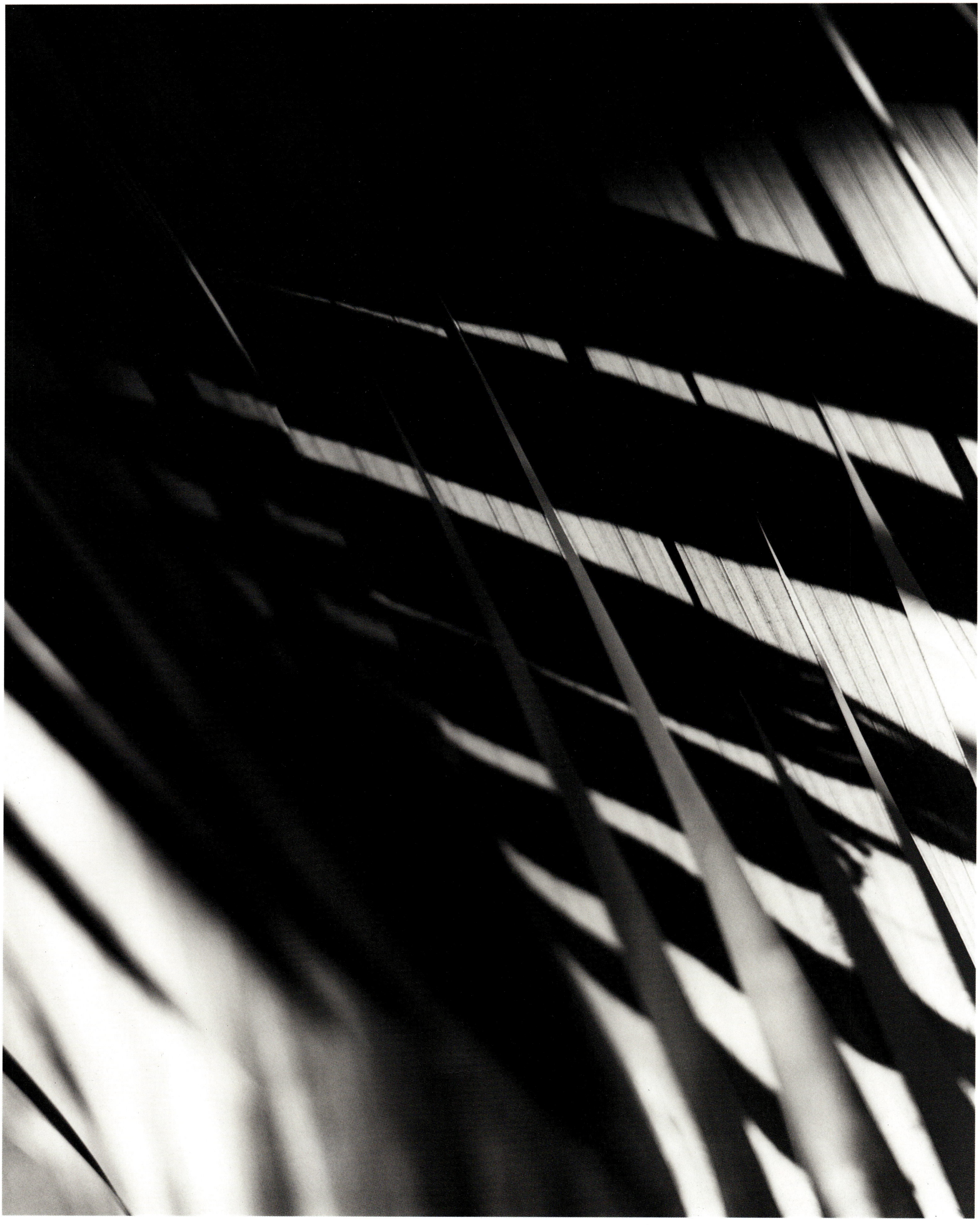

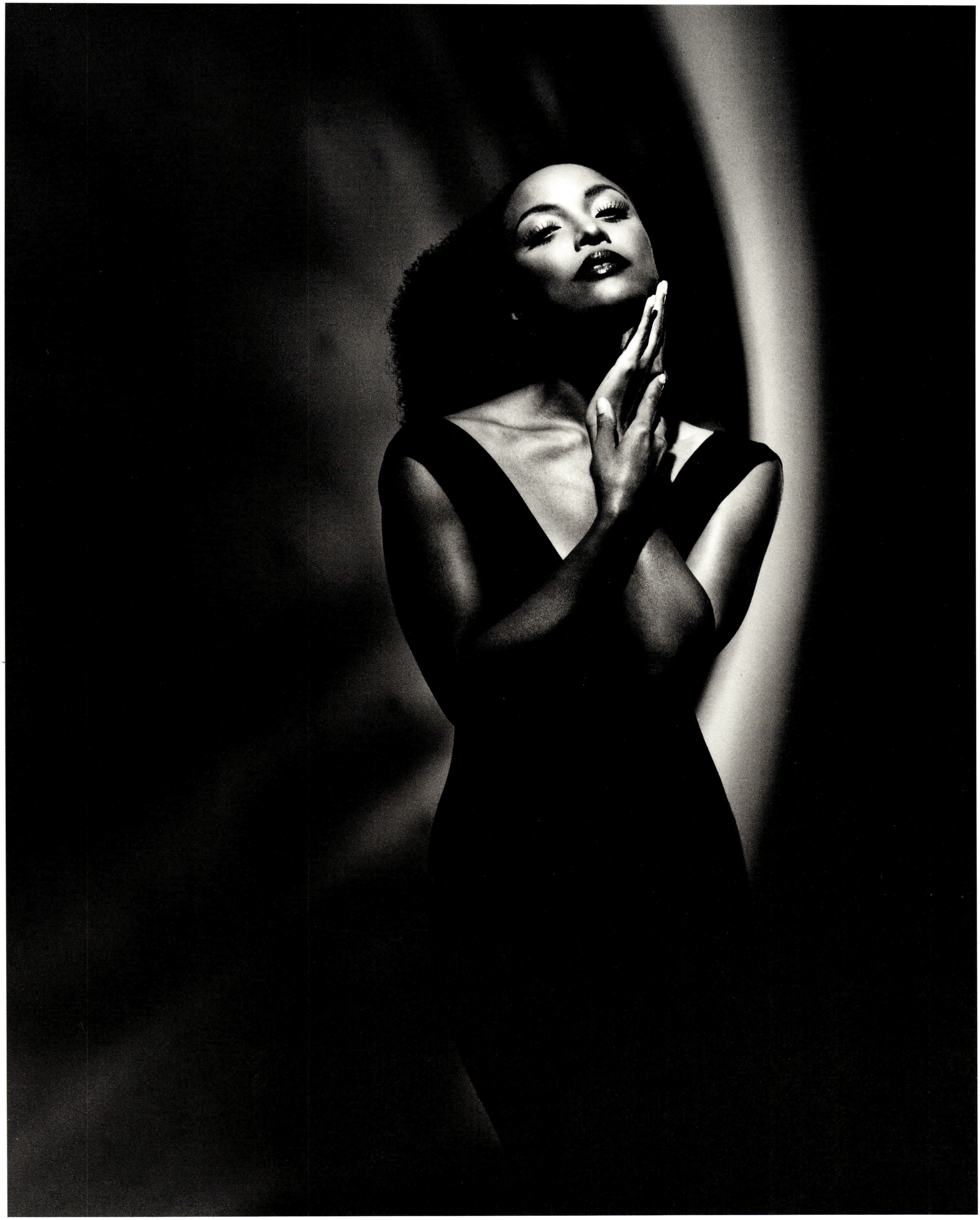

PRECEDING PAGES:

LEFT: PALM SHADOW, CHATEAU MARMONT, HOLLYWOOD, 1994

RIGHT: LYNN WHITFIELD, NEW YORK CITY, 1996

ROBERT PATRICK, CHATEAU MARMONT, HOLLYWOOD, 1994

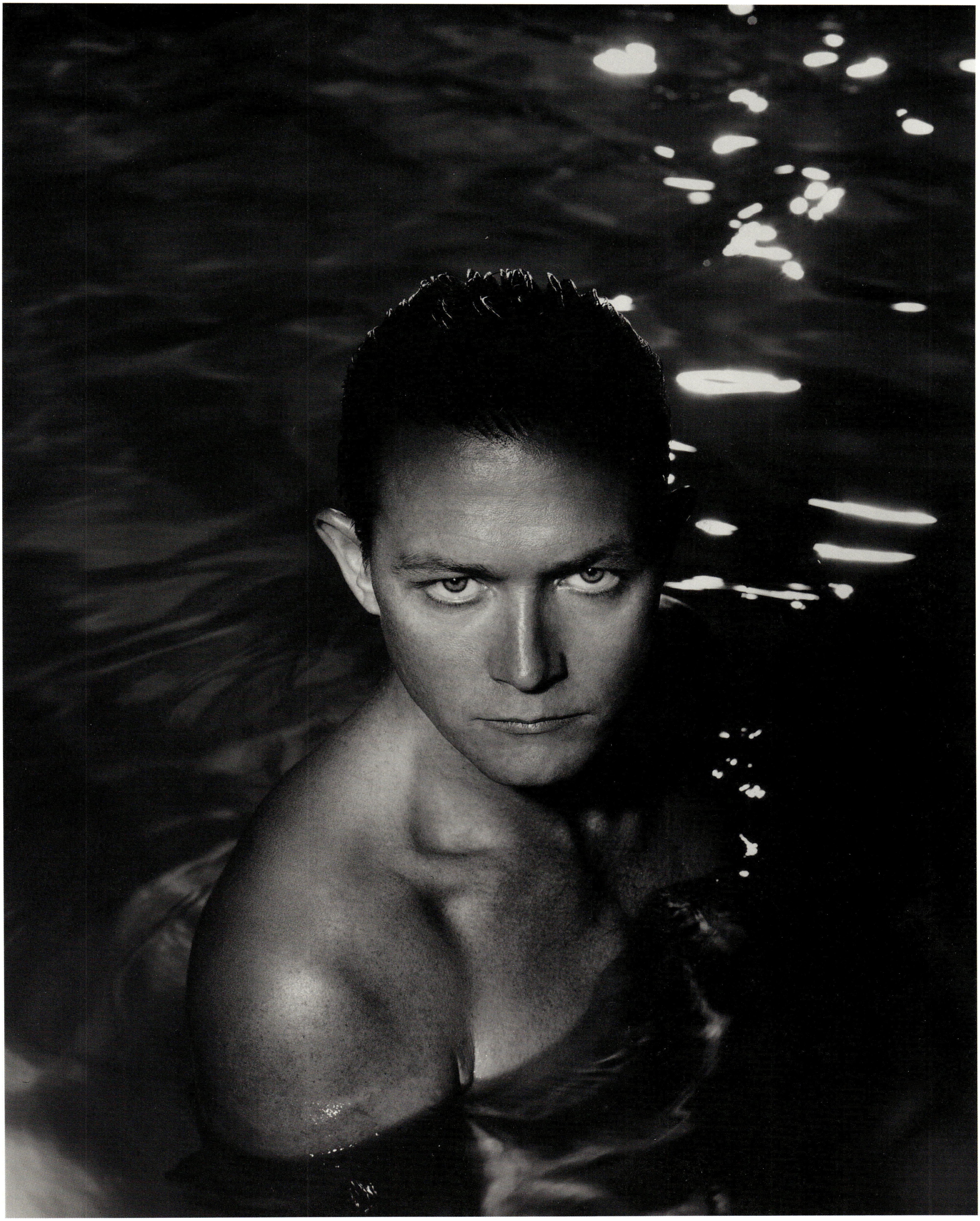

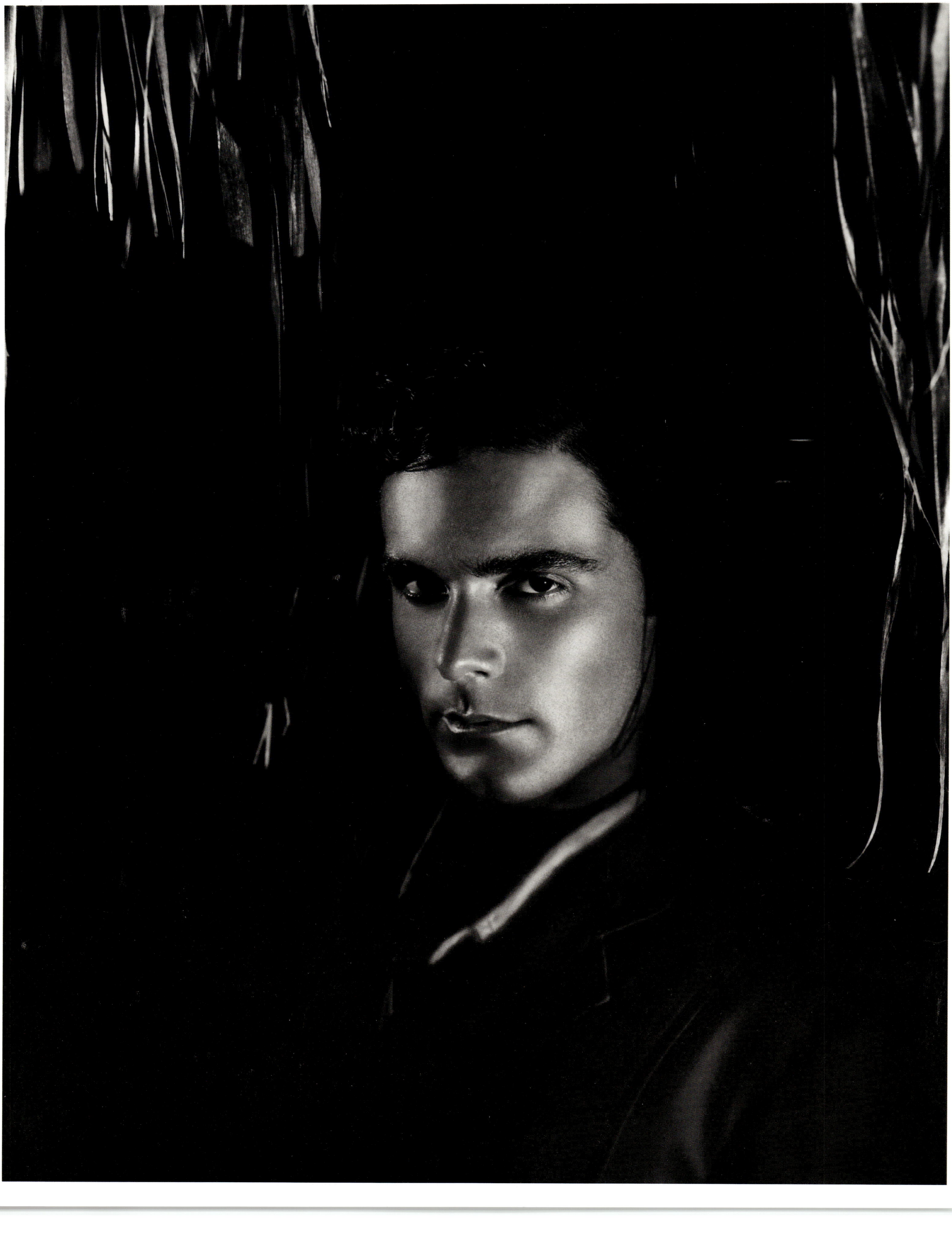

PETER DAVENPORT, "HERON'S NEST" ESTATE, BERMUDA, 1995

ERIC ROBERTS, CHATEAU MARMONT, HOLLYWOOD, 1994

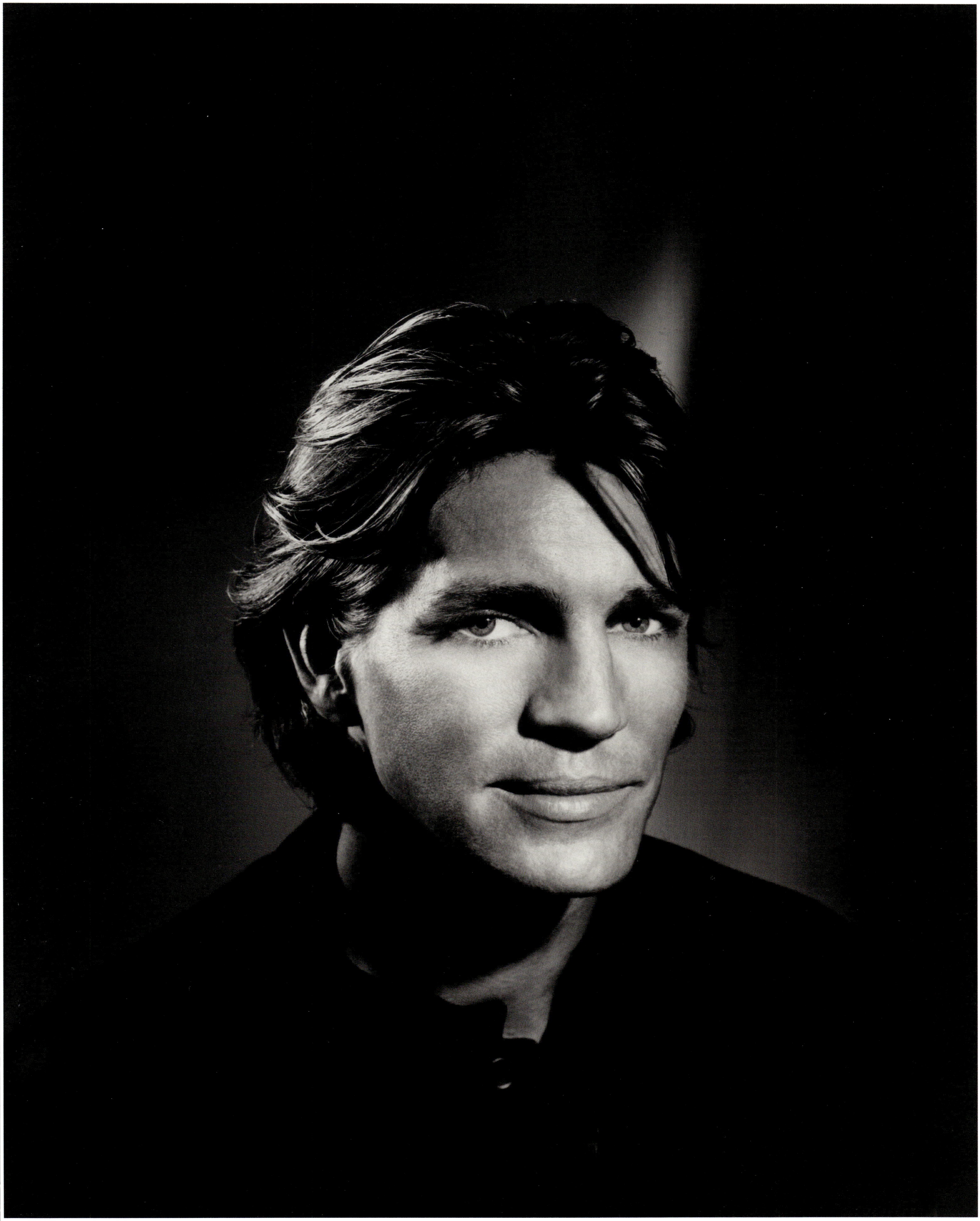

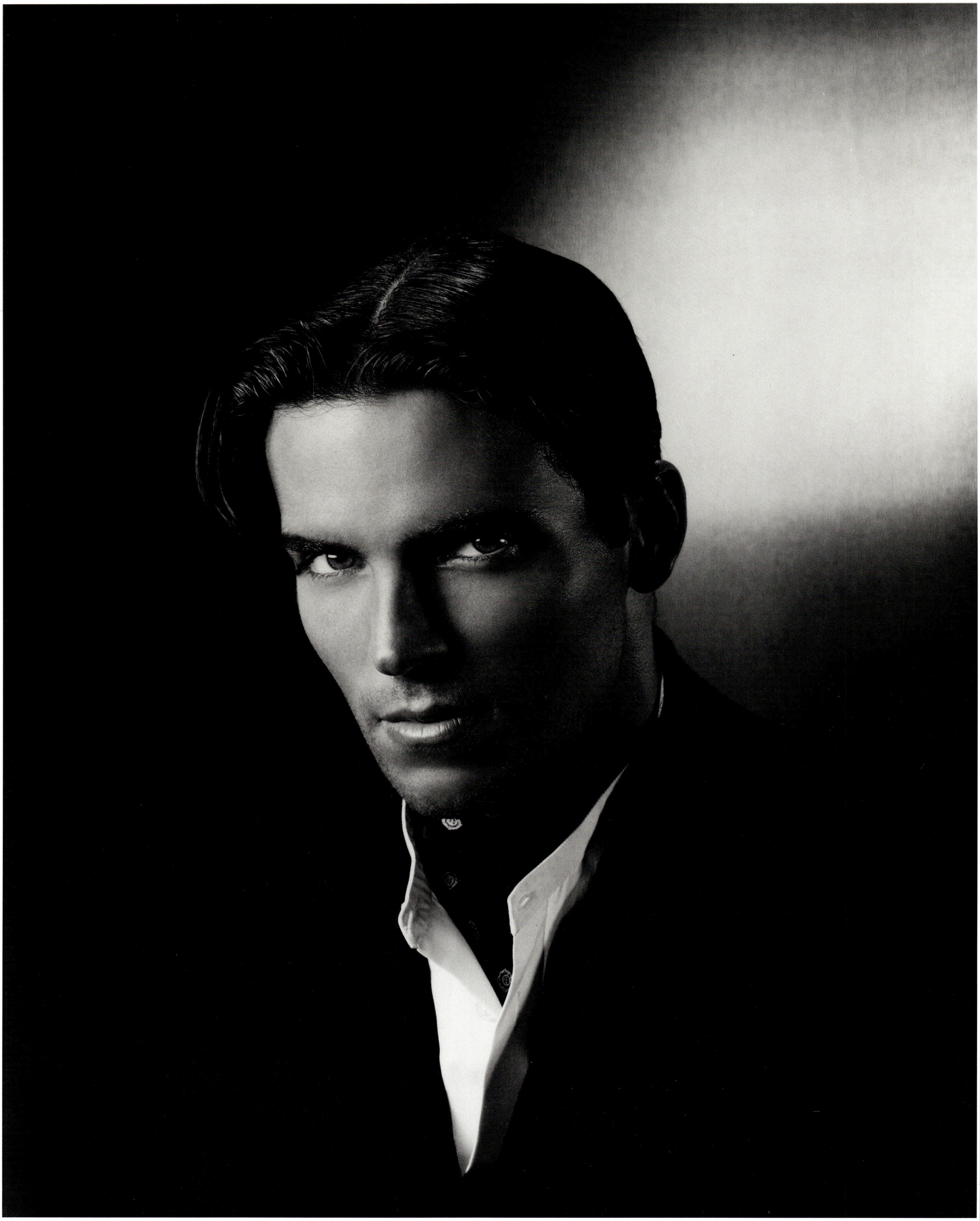

CHRISTOPHER DOUGLAS, NEW YORK CITY, 1994

TIM DALY, CHATEAU MARMONT, HOLLYWOOD, 1994

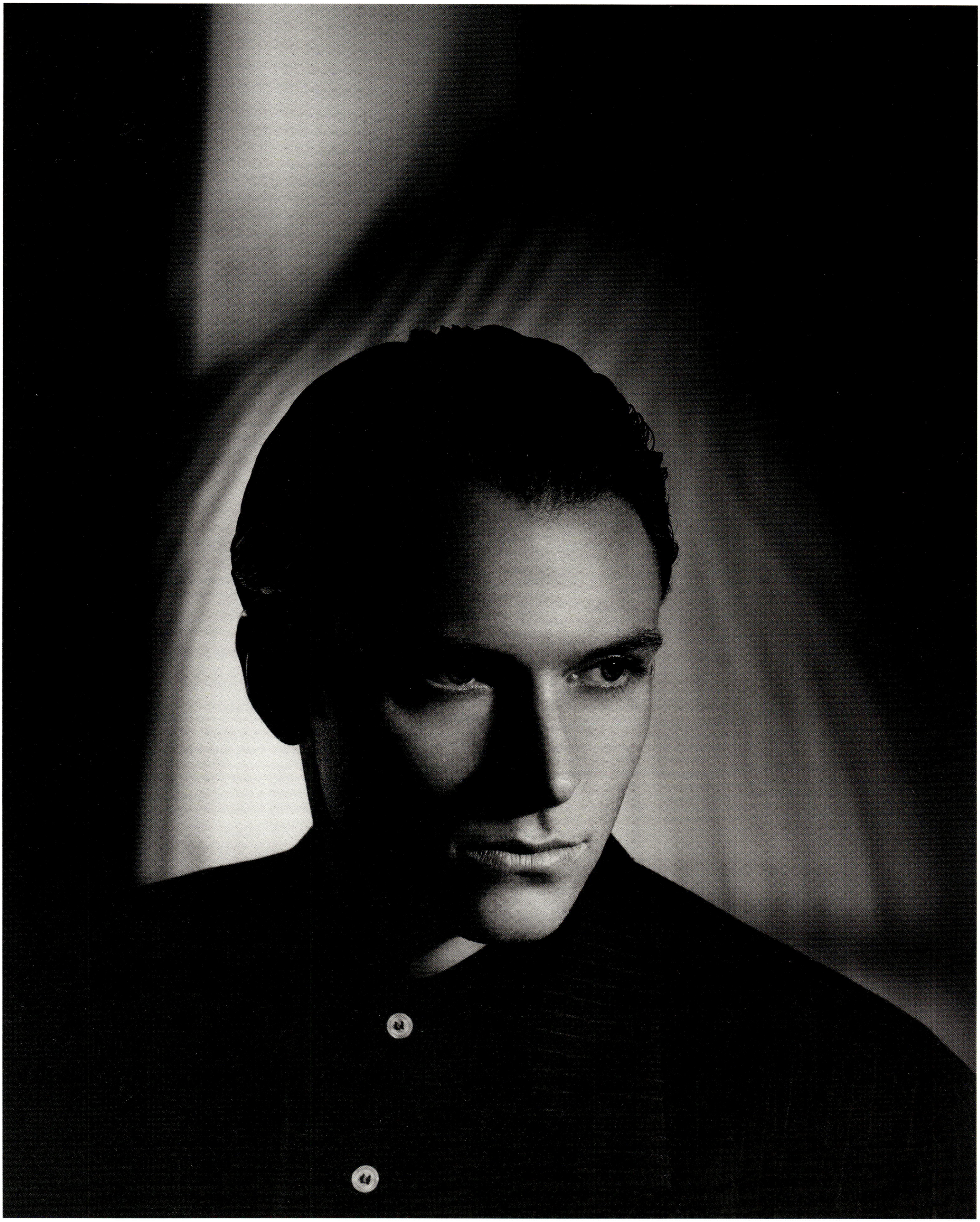

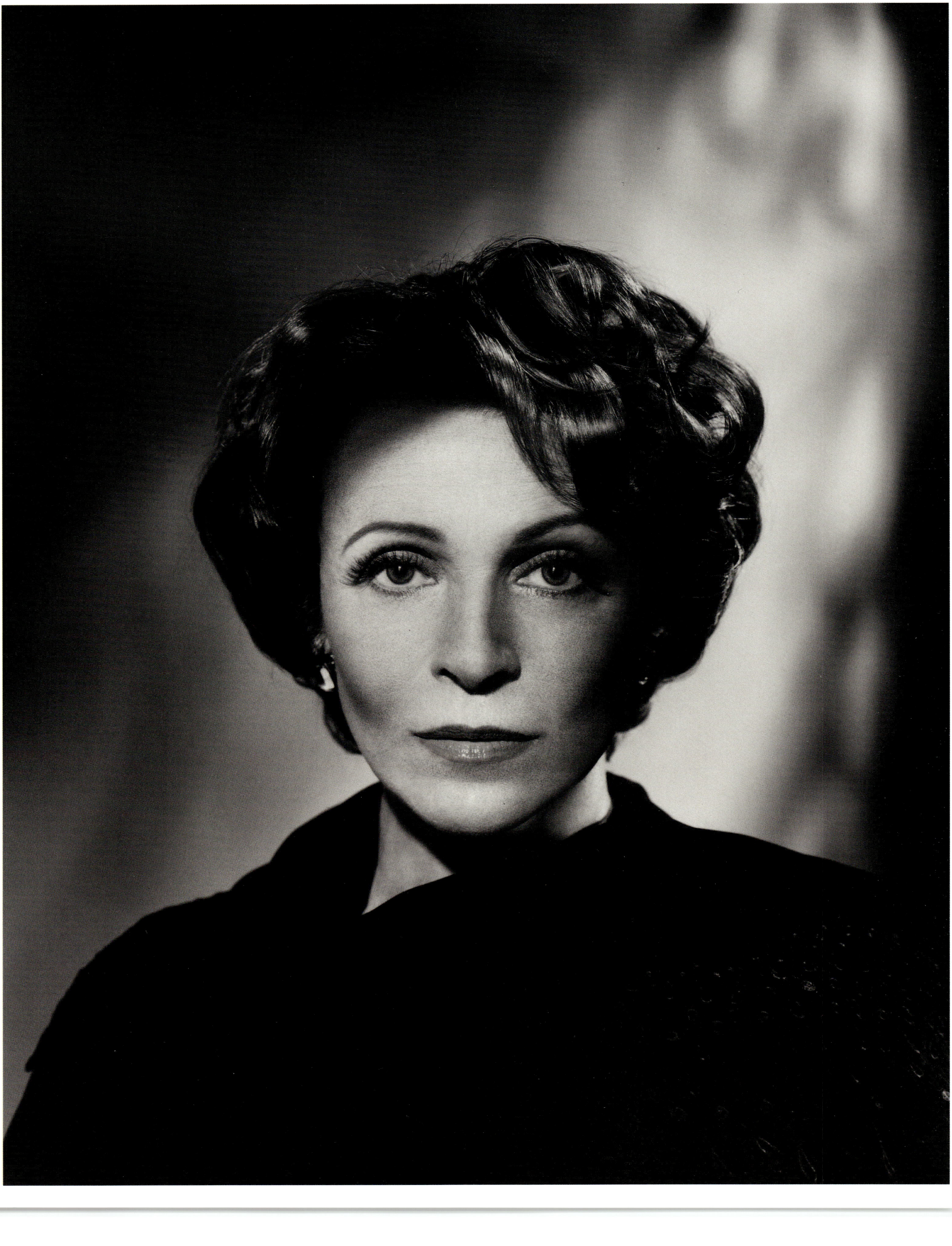

CLAIRE BLOOM, NEW YORK CITY, 1996

GRIFFIN DUNNE, NEW YORK CITY, 1994

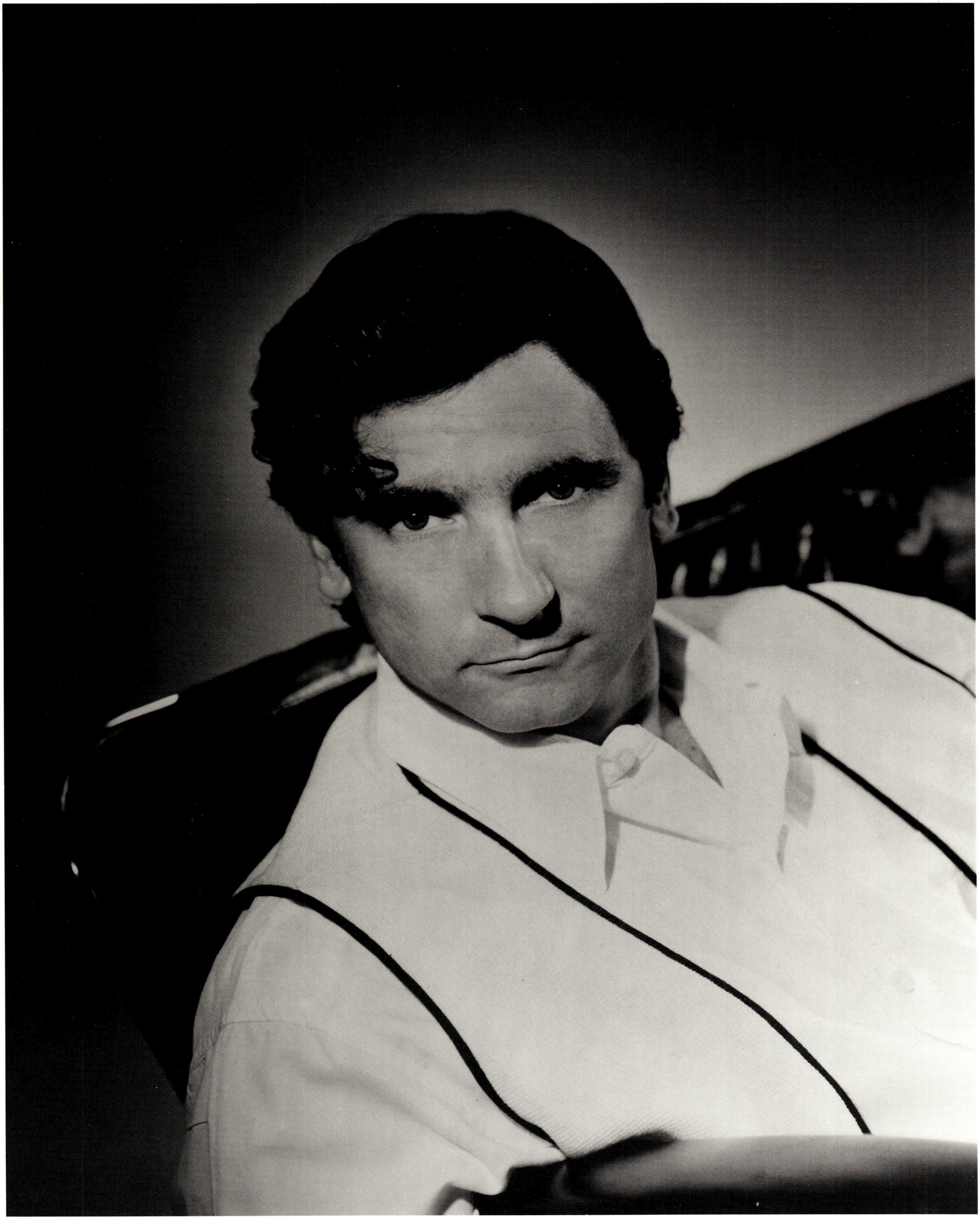

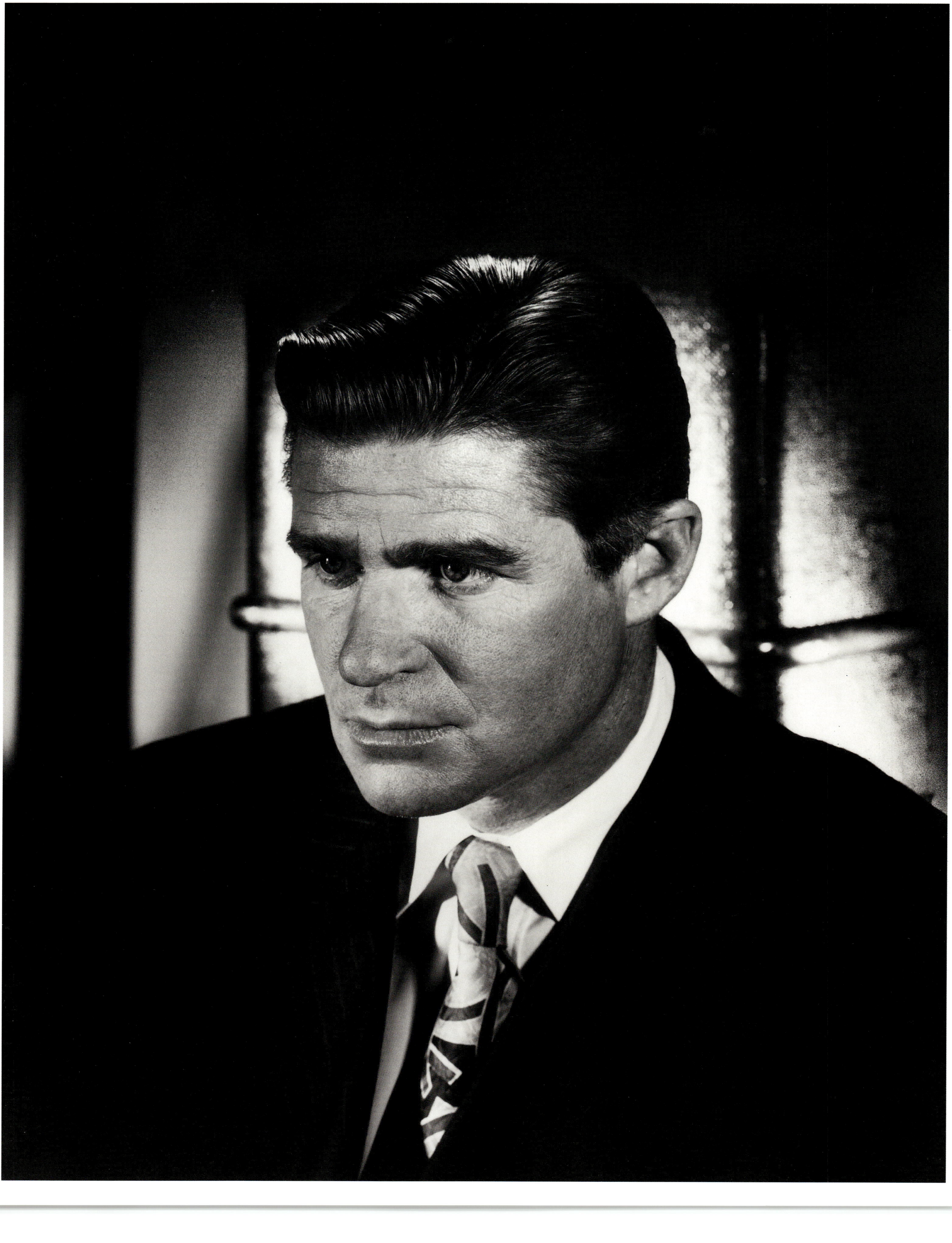

TREAT WILLIAMS, NEW YORK CITY, 1996

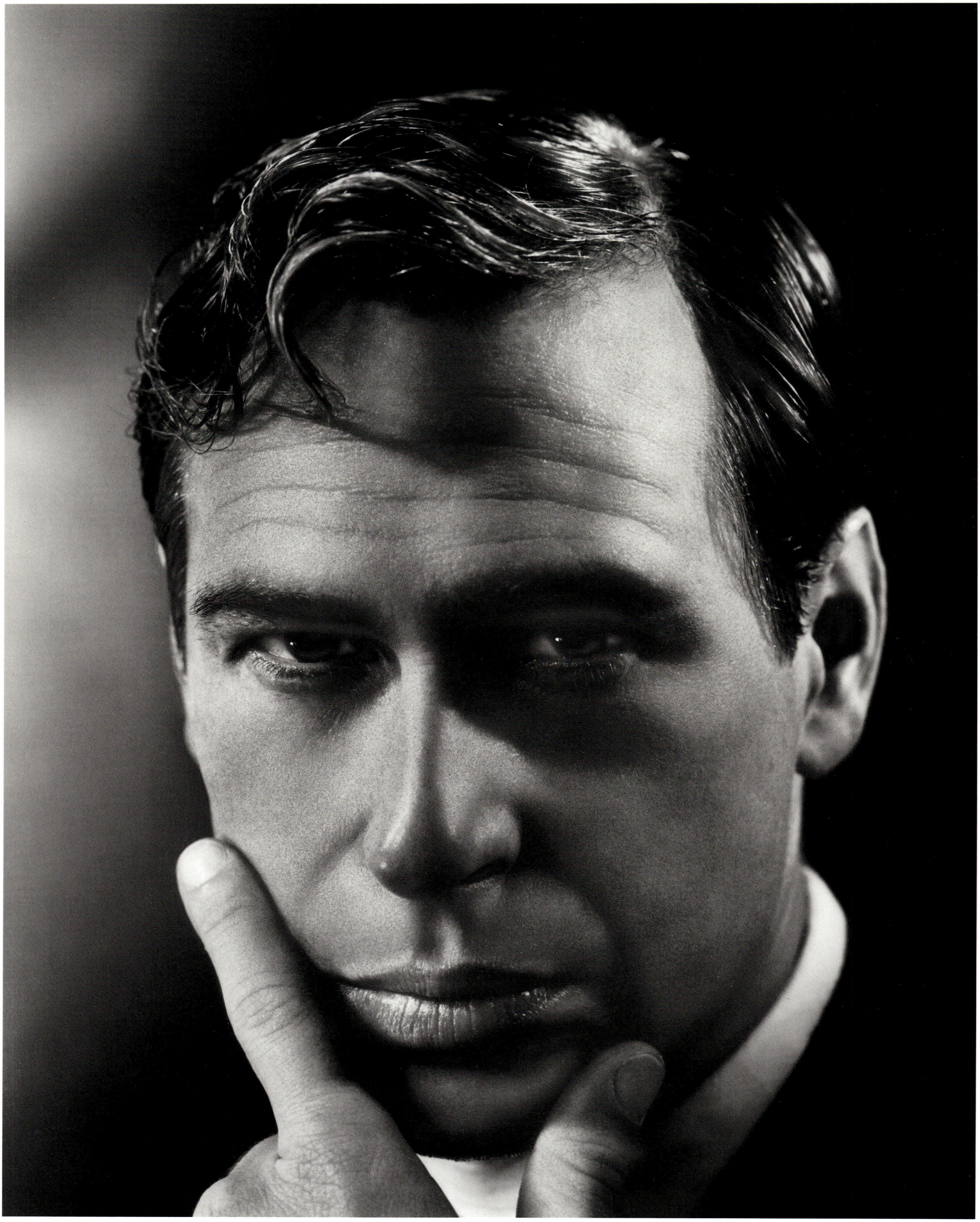

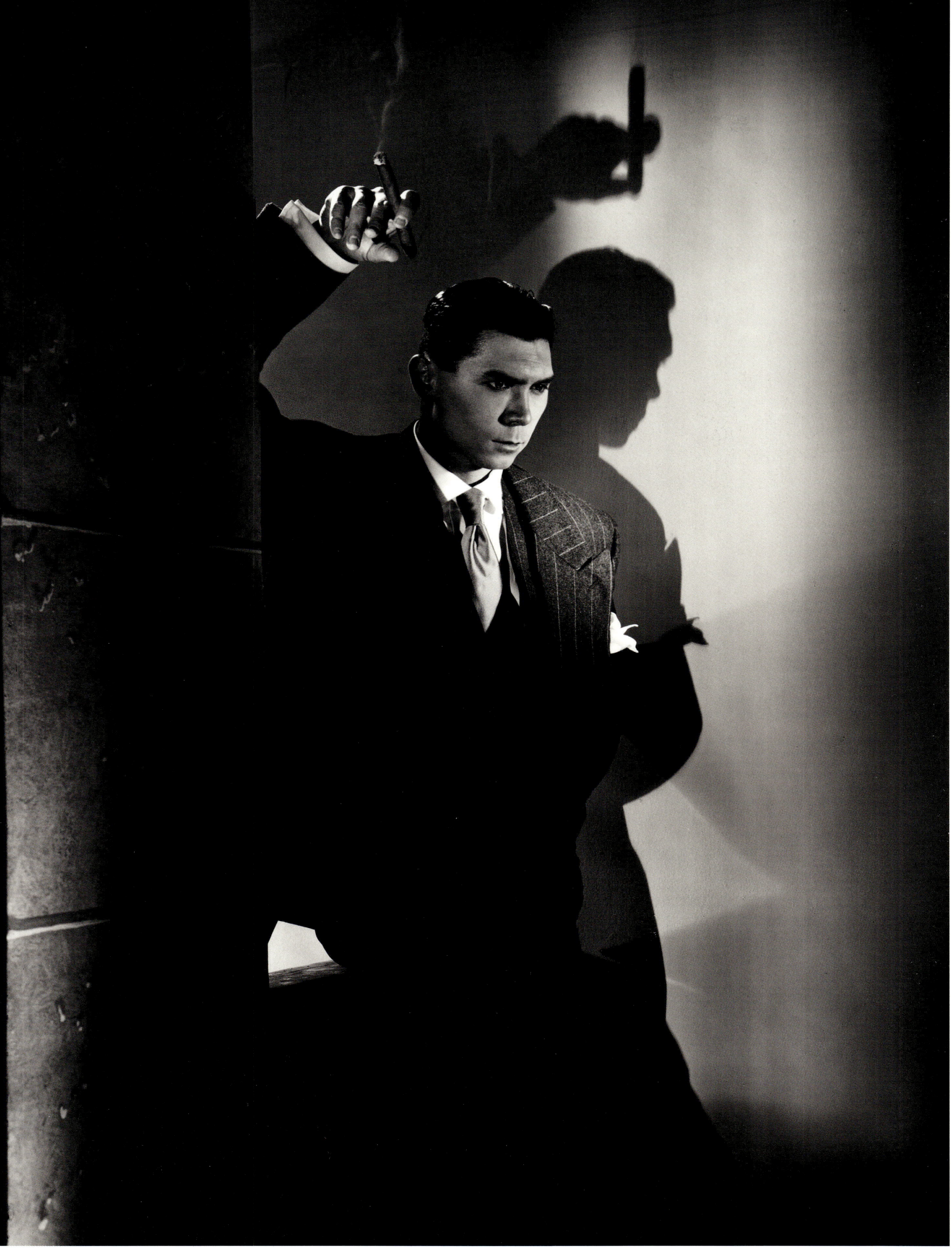

PRECEDING PAGES:

LEFT: SCOTT THOMPSON, NEW YORK CITY, 1995

RIGHT: LOU DIAMOND PHILLIPS, NEW YORK CITY, 1996

DOLPH LUNDGREN, NEW YORK CITY, 1994

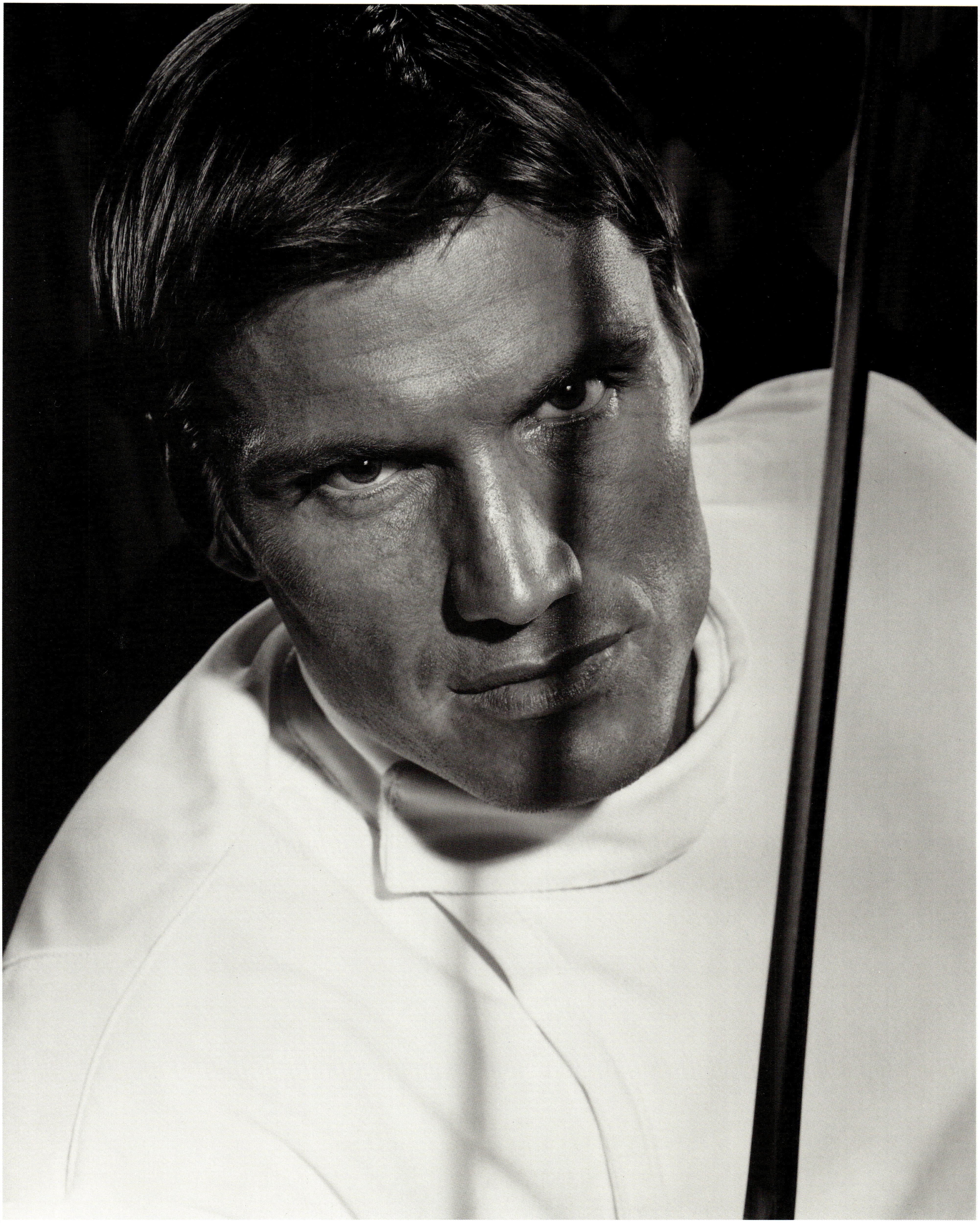

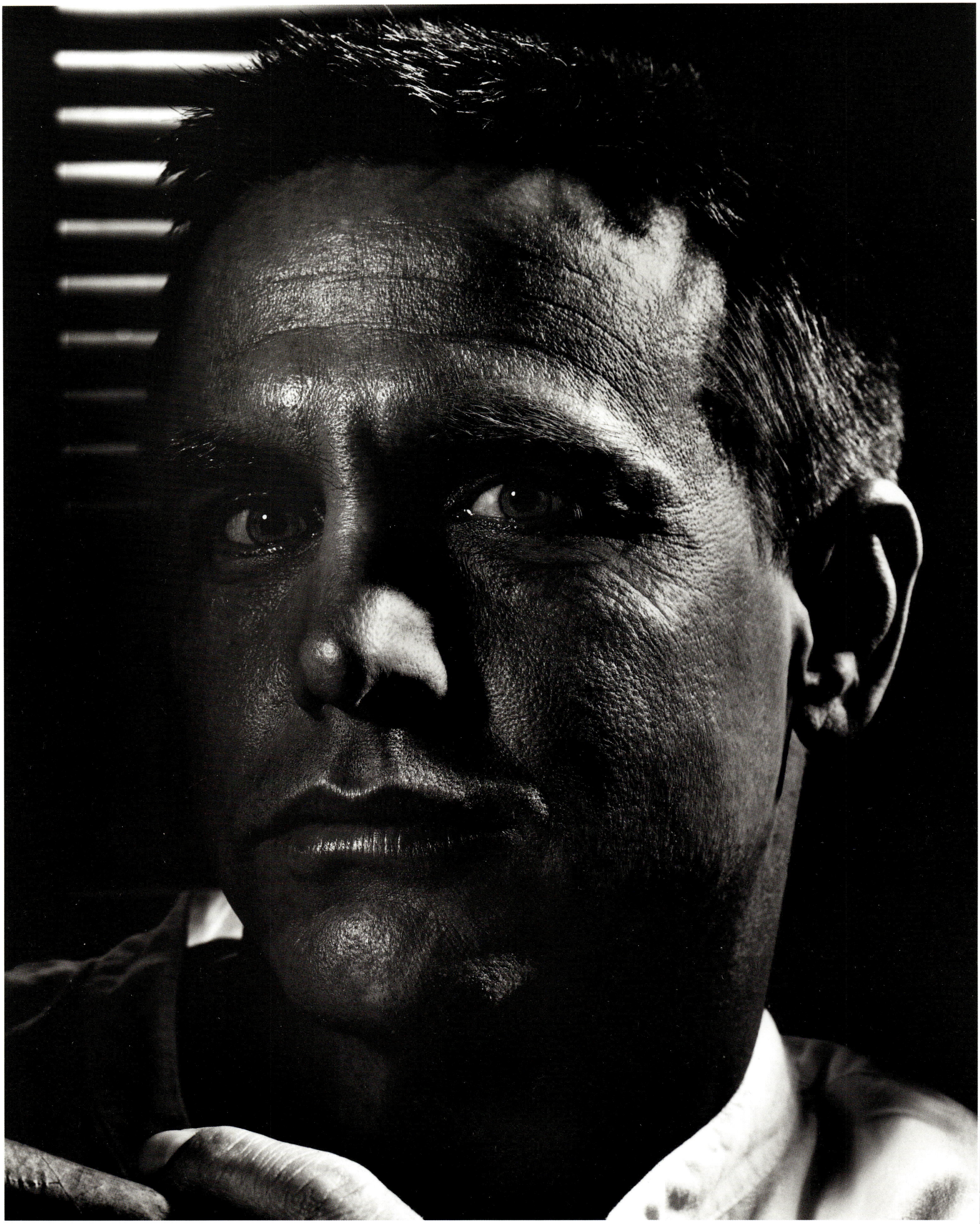

DAVID ANDREWS, CHATEAU MARMONT, HOLLYWOOD, 1994

PATRICK STEWART, NEW YORK CITY, 1995

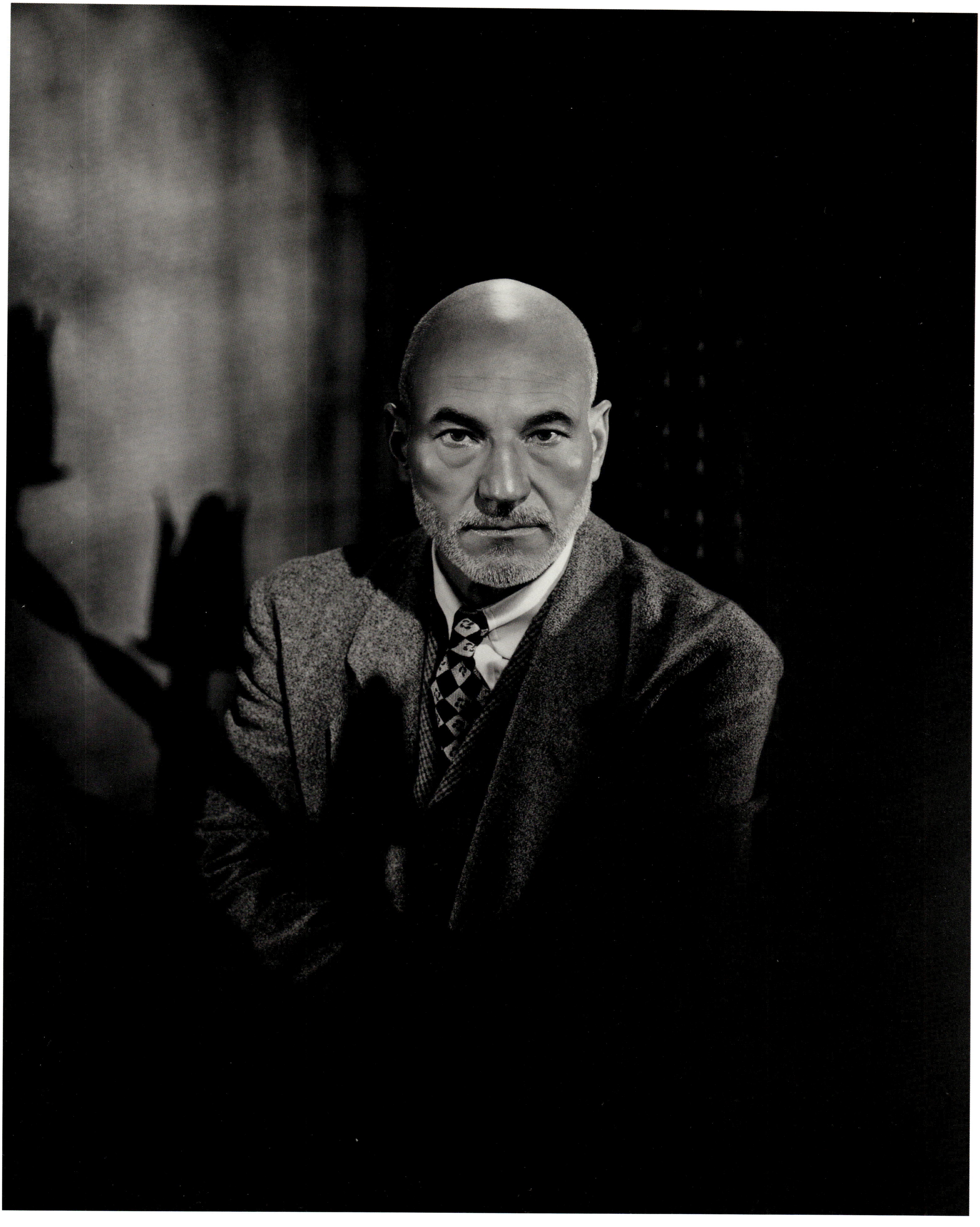

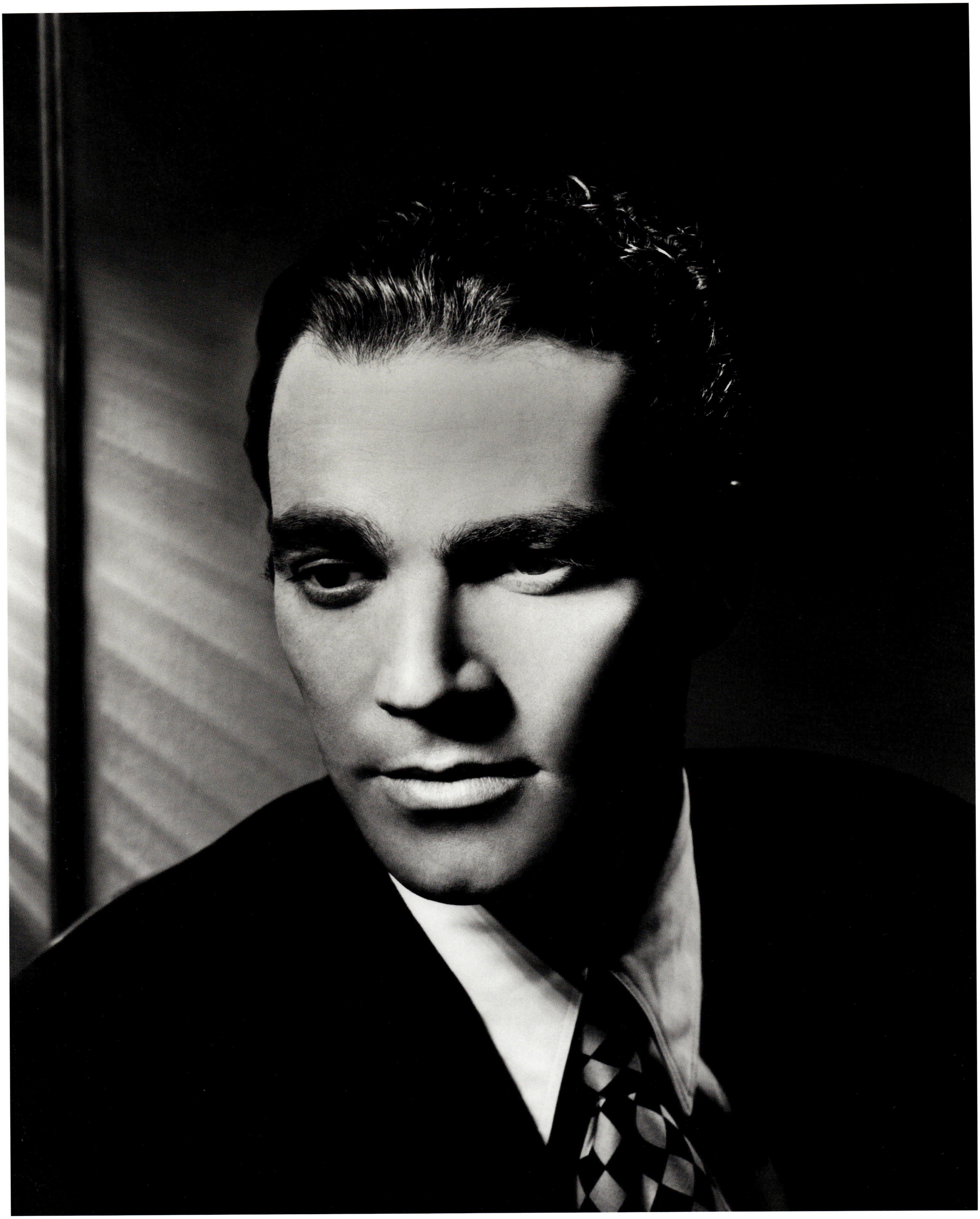

JON TENNEY, CHATEAU MARMONT, HOLLYWOOD, 1994

JACK LEMMON, STUDIO 70/70 C, HOLLYWOOD, 1995

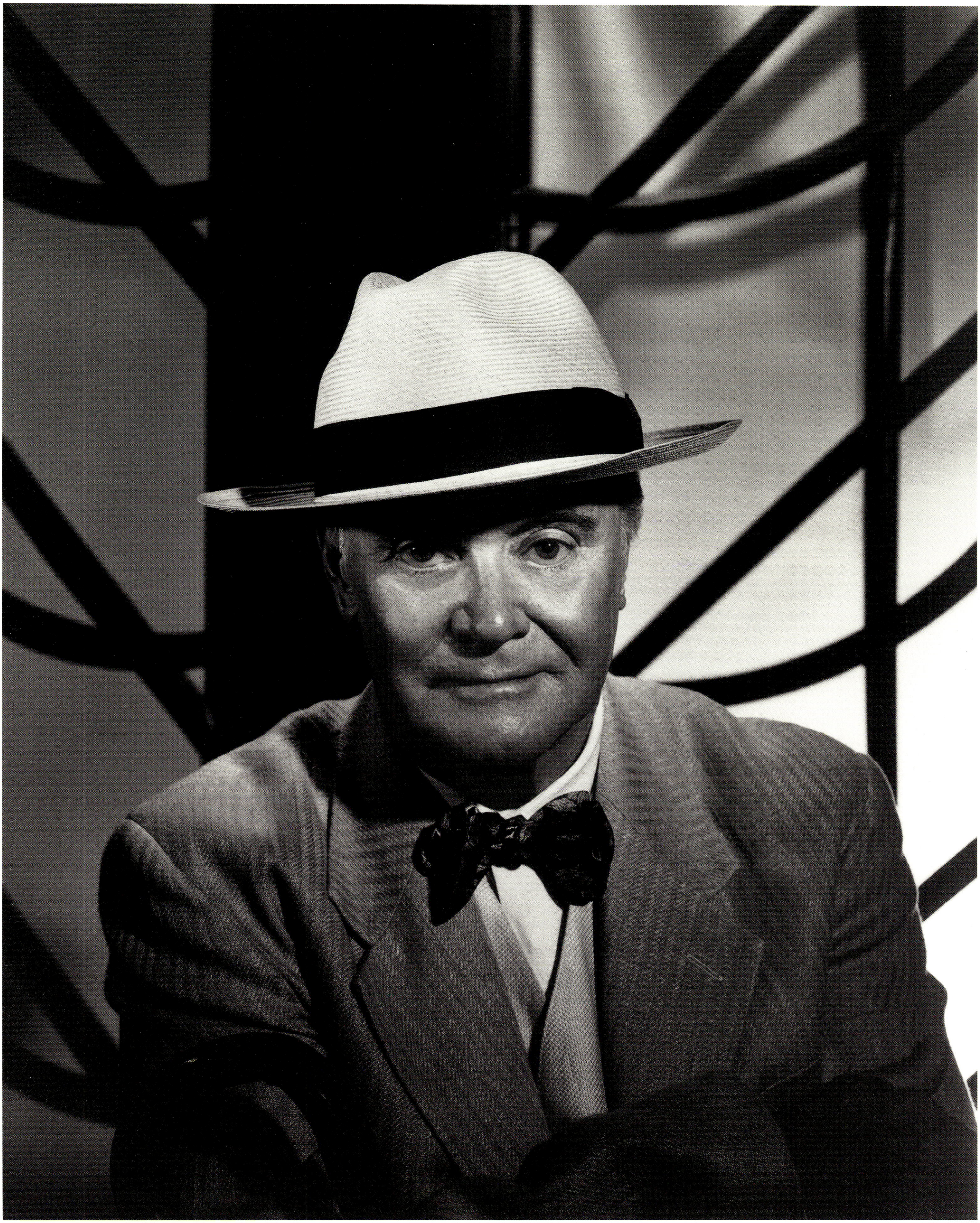

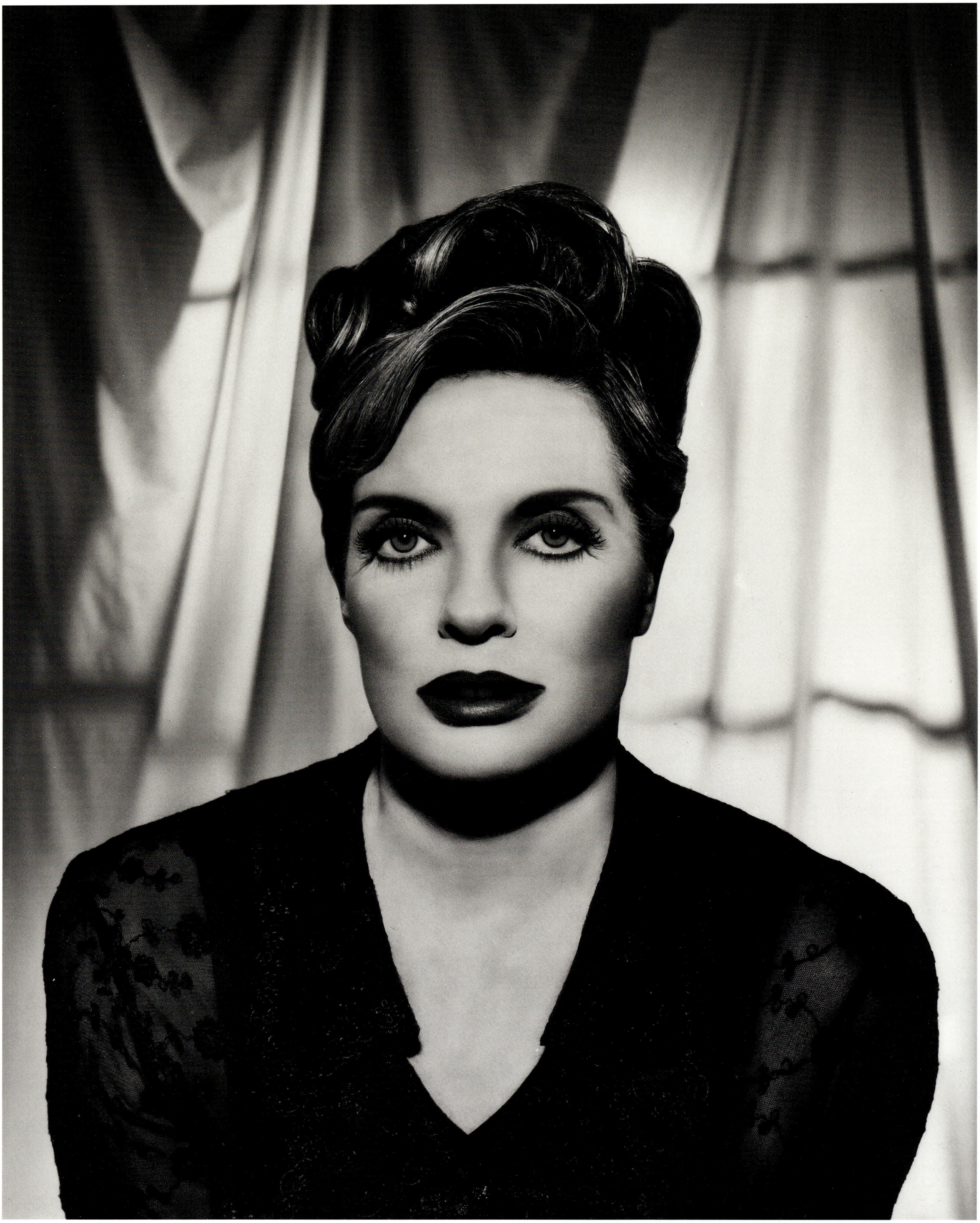

LINDA GRAY, CHATEAU MARMONT, HOLLYWOOD, 1994

LOU REED, NEW YORK CITY, 1997

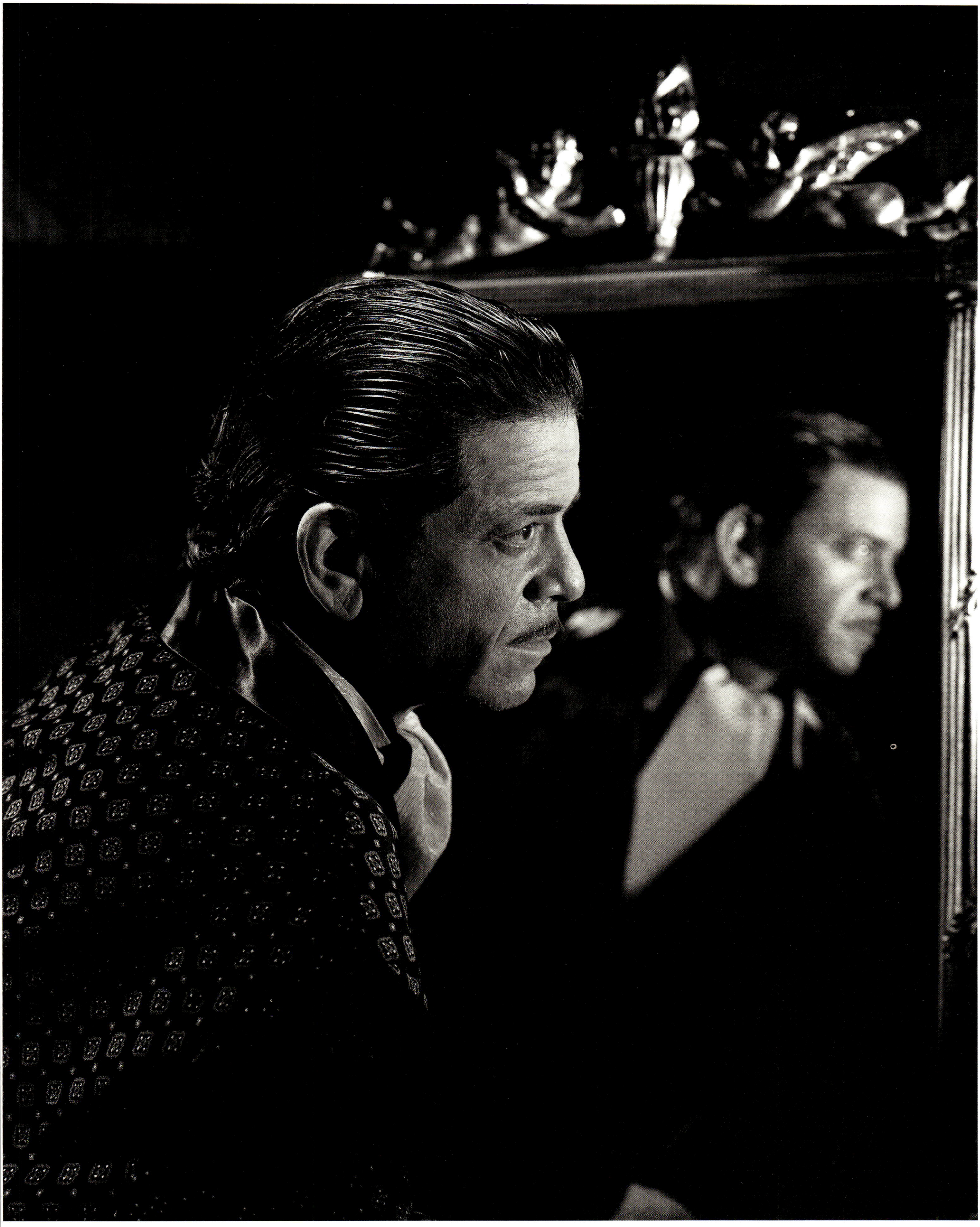

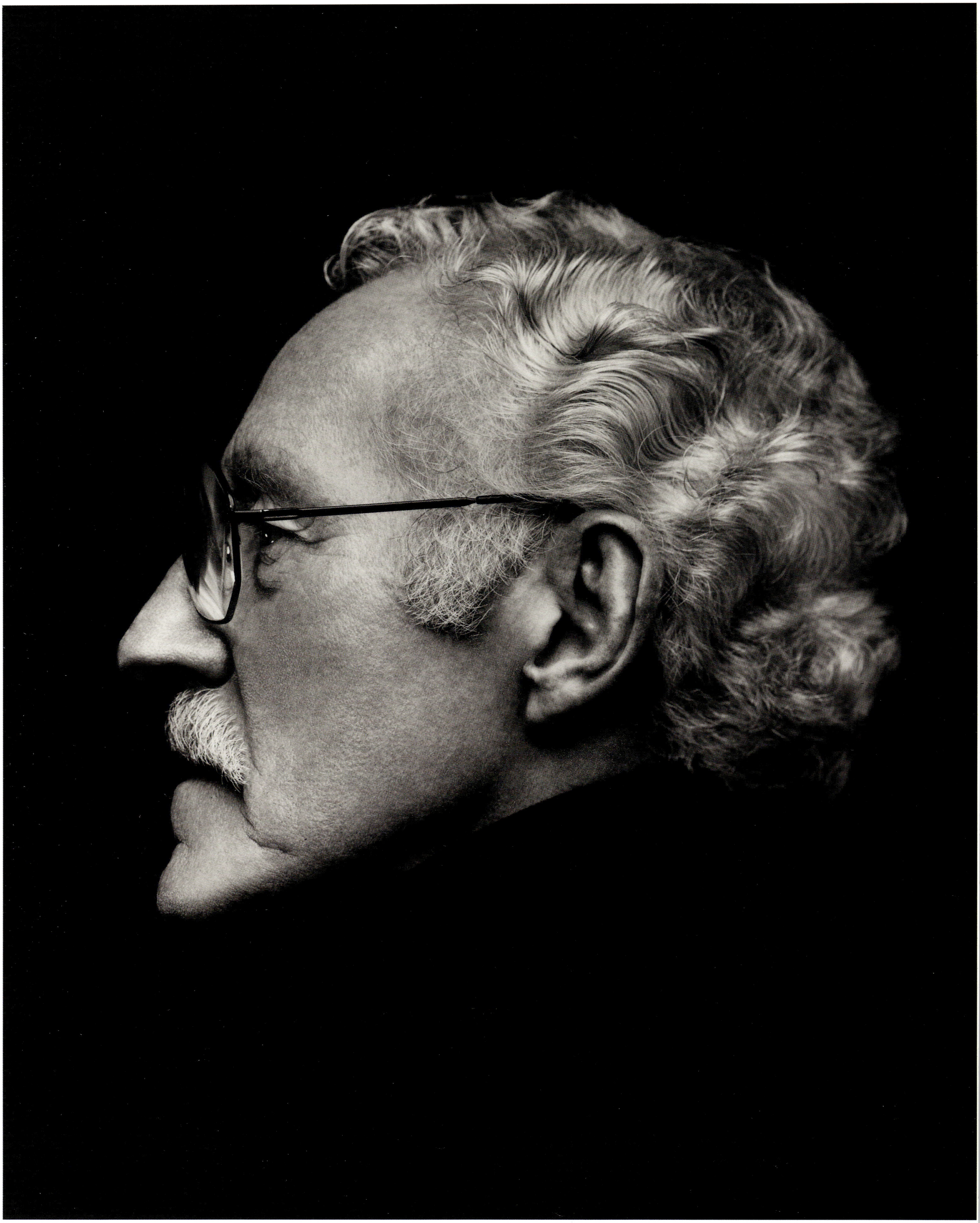

WILLIAM CLAXTON, STUDIO 70/70 A, SANTA MONICA BOULEVARD, 1995

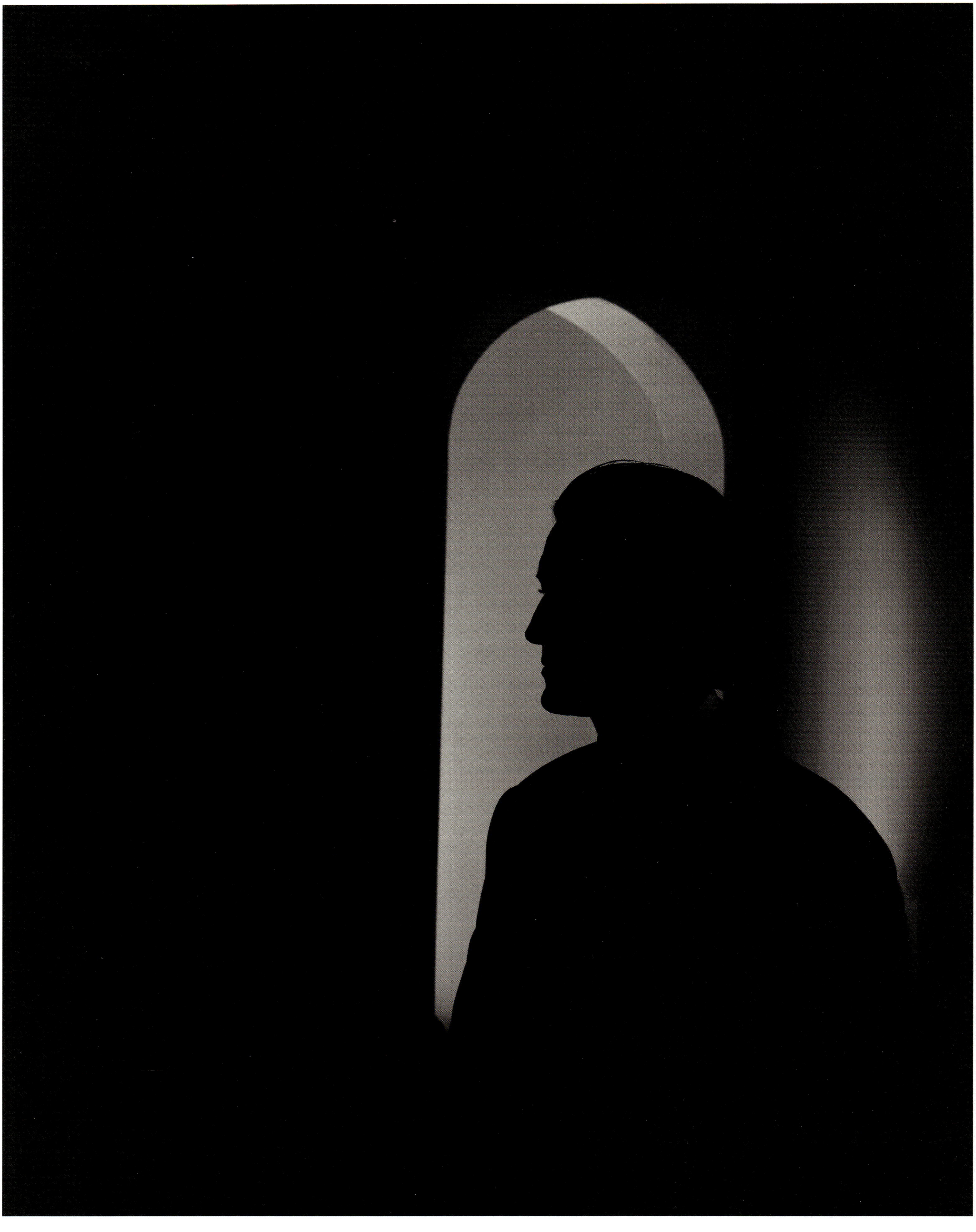

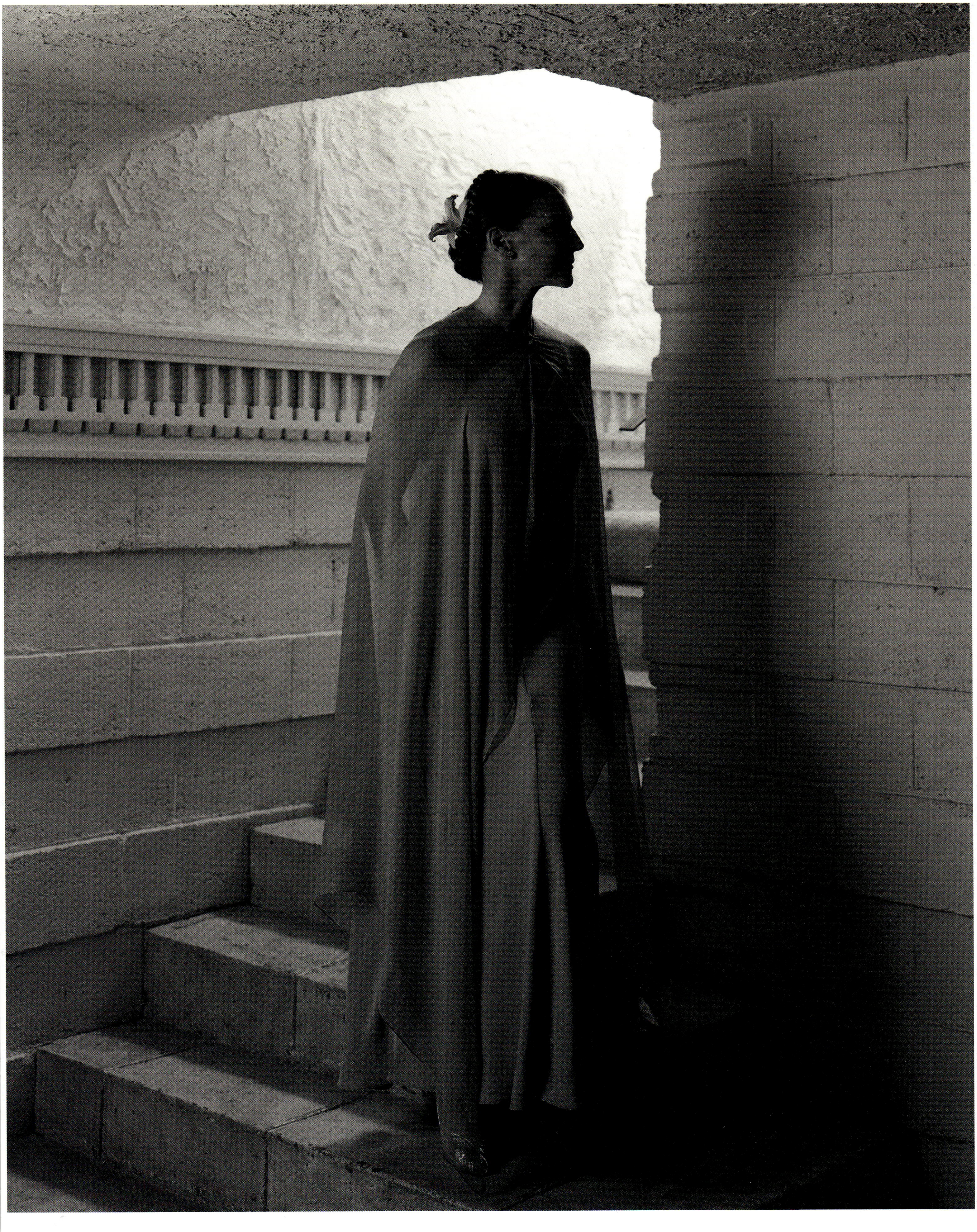

PRECEDING PAGES:

LEFT: PERRY KING, CHATEAU MARMONT, HOLLYWOOD, 1994

RIGHT: MIMI LONDON, HOLLYWOOD, 1994

ANN MAGNUSON, UNION STATION, LOS ANGELES, 1994

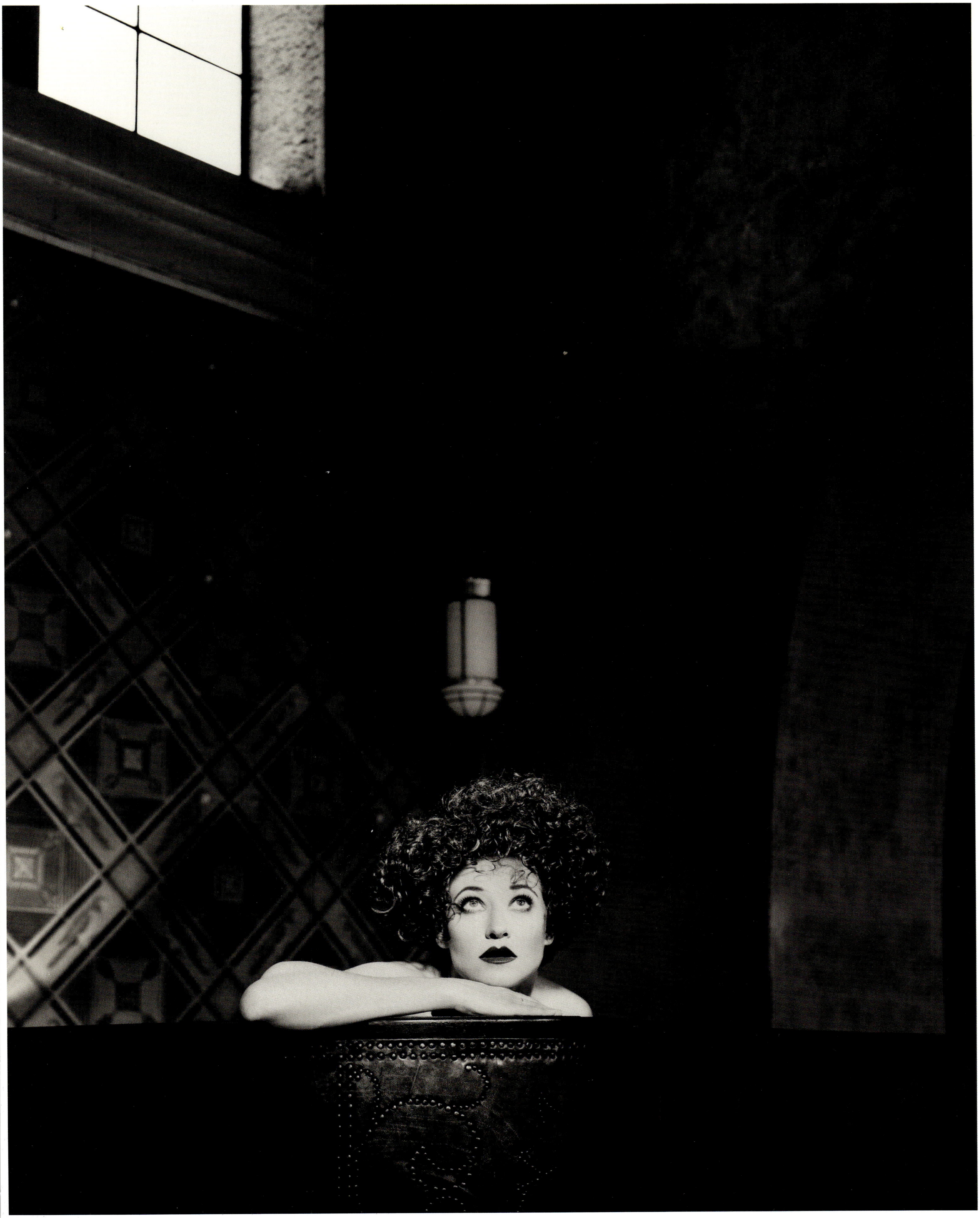

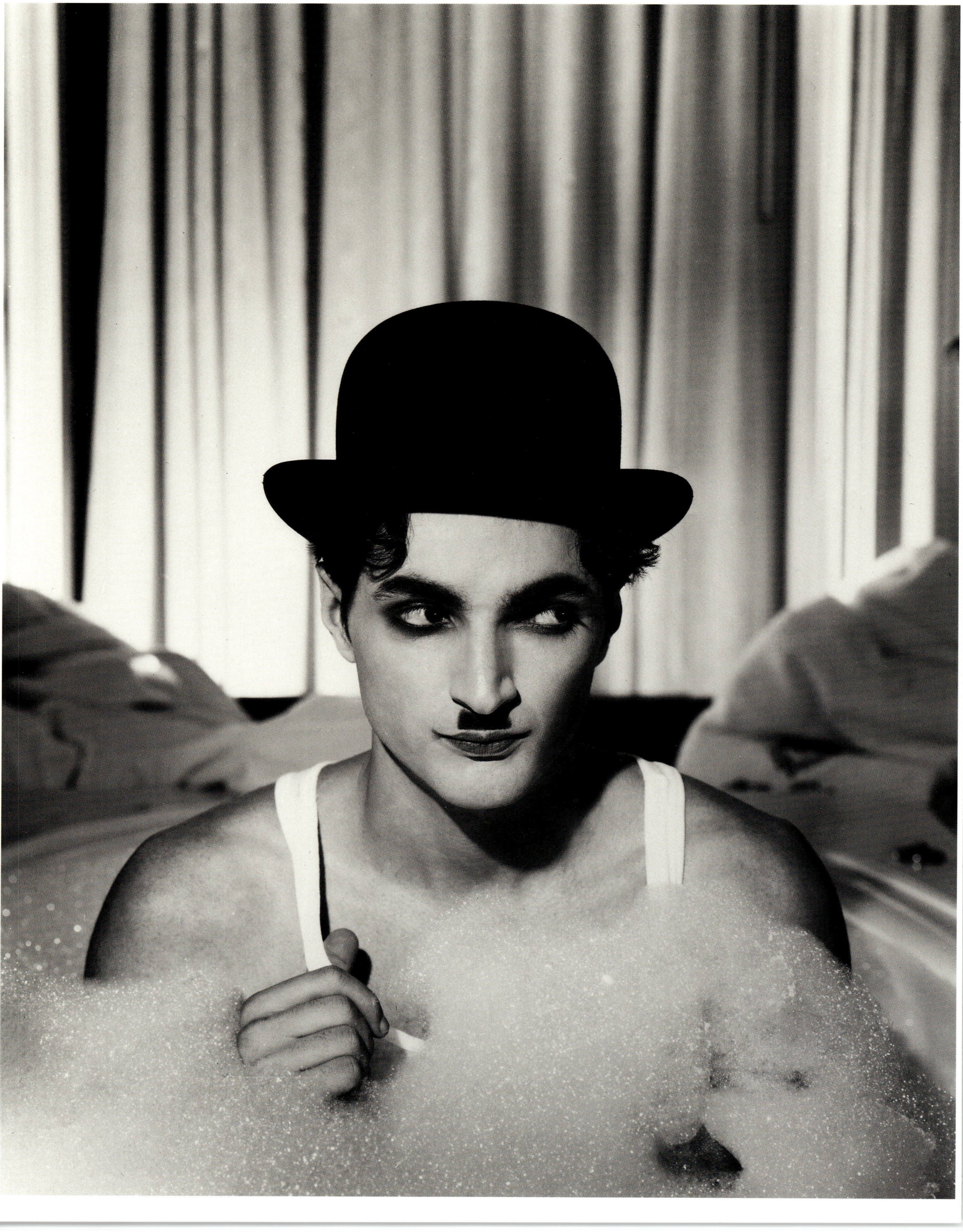

ROGER MOENKS, PLAZA HOTEL, NEW YORK CITY, 1996

MISS PIGGY, NEW YORK CITY, 1996

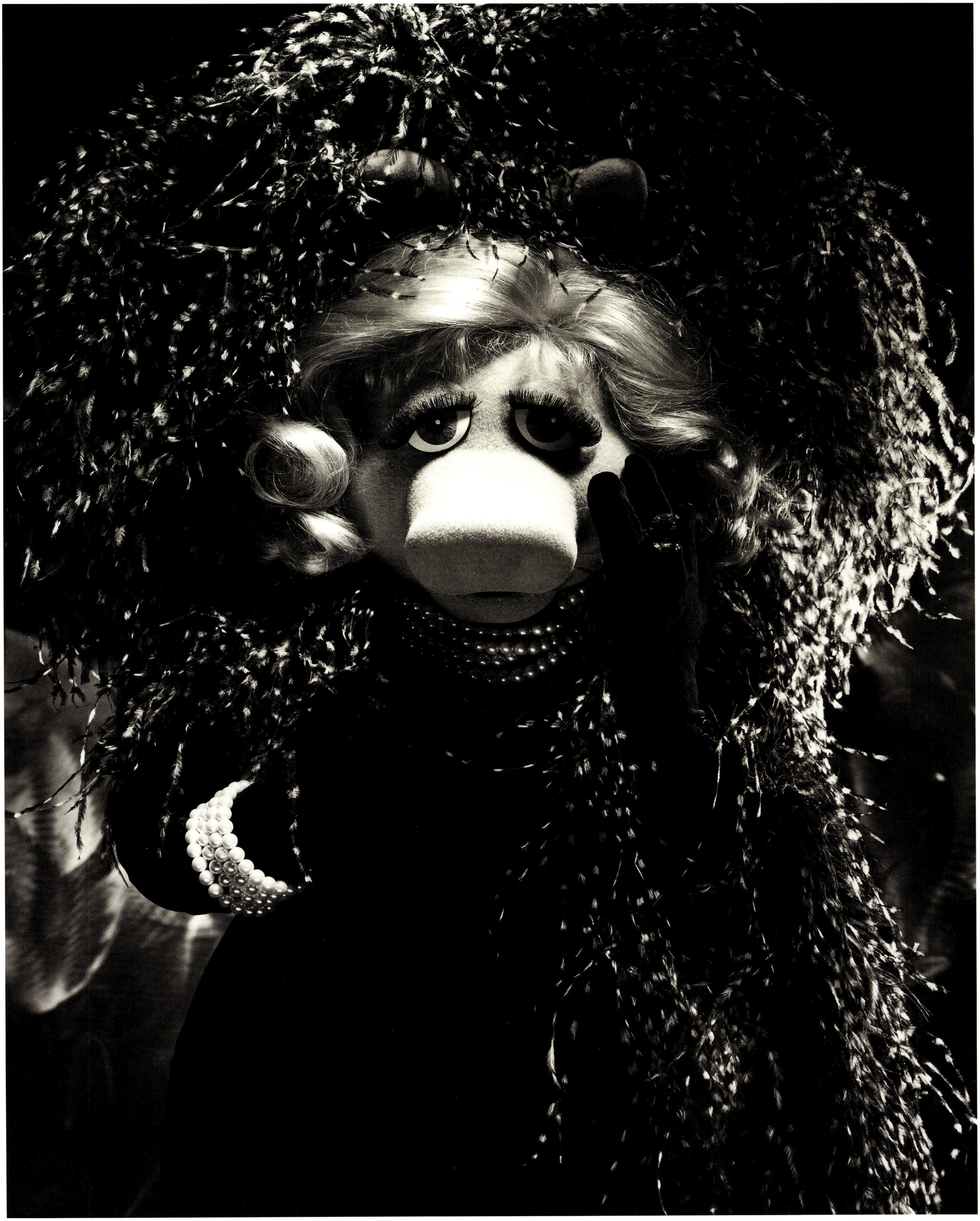

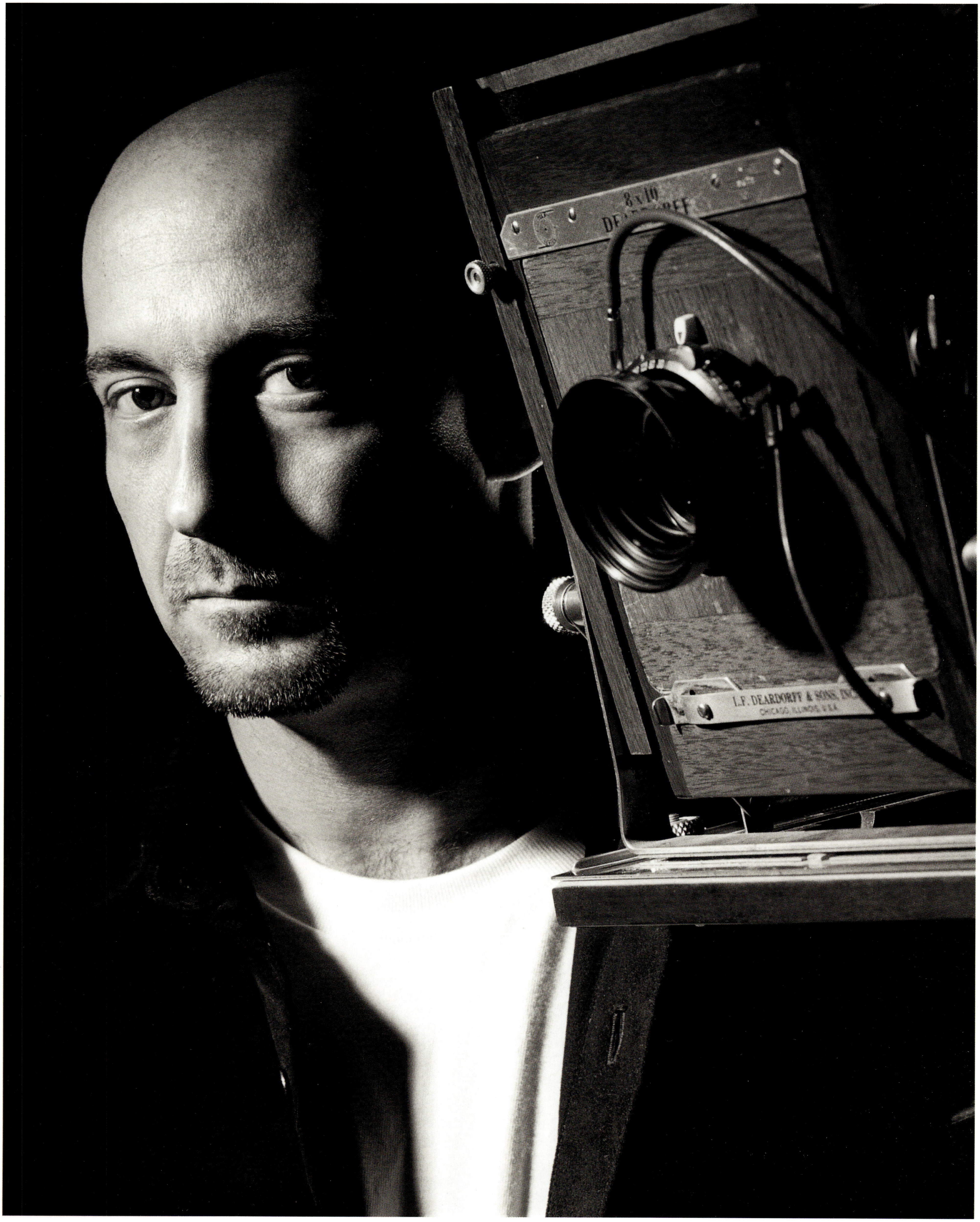
8 x 10
L.F. DEARDORFF & SONS, INC.
CHICAGO, ILLINOIS, U.S.A.

PHOTOGRAPHER'S AFTERWORD: In February 1994, I started photographing the movie, television, and fashion stars you see in this book in the style of the 1930s and 1940s golden-era movie images. I have always been impressed with the simple yet classic style of that period. I think every high-profile photographer working today owes a debt of gratitude to the individuals who created work in this genre.

To undertake this project I moved into the legendary Chateau Marmont hotel in Los Angeles with my business partner, West, and my photo assistant, Patrik. The style of the hotel was just what I needed—low-key with the right amount of historical reference for inspiration. My colleagues and I were a little tongue-tied those first few days. Inevitably, one of us would share an elevator or sit by the pool with someone whose work we admired from a distance—an actor, a musician, or a fellow photographer.

My first sitting for this project was on location from the top of Beverly Hills with the beautiful and gracious Kelly Klein. Kelly and I had run into each other several times at different functions. Like her husband, Calvin Klein, Kelly was mysterious. She was curious and kind, distant for privacy's sake, yet still open to me. She generously brought her own crew. Her makeup artist, Laura Mercier, and hairstylist, Didier Malige, are the absolute stars of their respective fields, but it was a personal assistant (unknown to me) by the name of Carolyn Bessette who would eclipse all of these personalities in only a few short years. I think back to that day with great fondness, snapping off a few casual photos of Carolyn while waiting for Kelly on the set. I heard the sirens that were going off around this woman, and I understood why John Kennedy Jr. became smitten with her.

More than a few people are surprised to learn that the creation of these highly stylized photos—made with an old wooden Deardorff 8"x10" view camera—required a down-and-dirty process behind the scenes. Many of these images were produced in our hotel suite at the Chateau Marmont. We improvised with back lighting over bedroom doors, hung sheets off the bed as background (much to the maid's bafflement), and created big-studio lighting in a nonstudio environment. Patrik would be on his hands and knees in a pitch-black closet trying to load film. But it was the detail within the frame that mattered. For Nina Siemaszko, a silk pillow, a glued-on wig flown in from New York, and every single eyebrow plucked out of her head (much to the squeamishness of the crew) was the price of glamour.

I will never forget when Perry King walked onto the set with a goatee. West kept mumbling about the fact that King's short beard was not of the period, all the while prodding me to ask Perry to shave his face. Perry obliged, but on the condition that West and I shave our faces too. So in celebratory manner, we all shaved off half our beards, snapped off a quick Polaroid of Perry, shaved the other half off, and then proceeded with the rest of the shoot. I thought I'd never hear the end of it from West. "Yeah, that's easy for Perry King to do, he's a dashing actor with or without a beard. I won't be able to get a date for another two weeks," he grumbled for the next three days. West now has second thoughts before suggesting eleventh-hour decisions on the set.

It's funny that in photography, art is made within the confines of an ordinary working day. This became clear to me on the day Dominick Dunne came to the studio to be photographed for an assignment for *Vanity Fair*. I think the picture I took of him was the exact essence of what I thought of him, as a great chronicler of a more glamorous period in history, but always the keen observer. Dominick had one great small trick up his sleeve during his shoot. As we left the dressing room to go to the set, Dominick removed a crumpled old reporter-style hat from his pocket. He was completely prop-ready. There was very little for me to do. Just a big light and the real man.

At one point I thought I would have given anything to bring back the old Hollywood that Dominick Dunne experienced firsthand. But I now realize that I have some classic stories of my own. Like the day Debi Mazar, who at the time was just starting out, agreed to sit for me, but only on the condition that I pay her enough money so she could pay her phone bill.

One of the more embarrassing moments came on the day Miss Piggy arrived for her sitting. For her shoot, we ordered a catered lunch for about eight people. Miss Piggy entered the studio with a handsome gentleman whom we all assumed was her latest paramour, and she gazed upon the beautiful spread of food. From what I gather, she assumed that the rest of the crew had eaten earlier and that the untouched food in front of her was *all* for her! Needless to say, none of the crew ate much of a lunch that day. I recall eating a single green grape that afternoon.

Peter Weller's image with the trumpet also brings back a wild flashback. For his shoot, I set out with my crew, Robert, the makeup man; Deborah, the stylist; West, Barbara, and my photo assistants Patrik and Astor for Peter's secluded retreat in the Hollywood Hills. We arrived at the house to find a speaker box that did not respond to our requests for entry. I gave instructions for everyone to wait in the cars while I slipped through a narrow opening in the gates to search for Weller in the hopes that I would find him somewhere on the property sunbathing or swimming. Just as I was about to give up, Peter Weller's black car pulled into the driveway. He invited us in, whereupon we were instructed that he wanted "no makeup, no clothes" (which we had racks of, by the way); however, we were allowed to set up anywhere we liked. Just as we were set up to shoot the portrait, I heard the music of Miles Davis vibrating through the large house, but the subject of our photograph was nowhere in sight. I followed the sound, which led me to find Peter standing on a small carpet, in front of a huge painting, playing his trumpet along with Miles on the stereo. Seeing Weller at that moment, I realized that the only way to photograph him was with his horn. I spied a beret hanging on a closet doorknob and a smoky black sportjacket nearby. Weller agreed to the costume with an enthusiastic response. As Weller *finally* sat for the portrait with the horn against his cheek, his eyes practically burned through the camera lens, and his soul was mine for that brief and sought-after moment.

One of the more touching moments I remember occurred during the sitting with Calvin Klein. It took eight months of coordinating our schedules to arrange the shoot at the Pier 59 Studio in New York. True to style, this was the most austere studio I had ever seen. A glass wall framed a view of the Hudson River. Everything inside was white with a few embellishments of stainless steel. When Calvin arrived, he released his black garment bag at my feet and disappeared into the makeup artist's embrace. Calvin emerged makeup- and costume-ready in his black jacket and gray cashmere sweater. His face was radiant in the light that I created for him, and his posture was strong and confident. The moment we were about to shoot, the phone rang. It was a call from Calvin's office, but he could not move for fear of disturbing the set—a leather chair atop a large white box. Calvin's assistant requested a cellular phone number to transfer the important call to Calvin. A moment later my cell phone rang and my assistant, Meagan, said as she handed the phone over to Klein, "There's a call for you, Calvin. It's your mother." At that point I was able to connect that experience with our final photograph of Calvin, in the pose of Rodin's *Thinker*, with thoughts of his mother.

In hindsight I am fascinated by the incestuous nature of how some of these shoots came together. One thing truly does lead to another. For me, this project was never about the caliber of the celebrity. It was about the essence of a more romantic period we may never see again. Some memories have a haze and some have a glow, but I always choose to remember the latter. Retracing my footsteps from the moments that make up this collection, I realize that my art for this project has also been my joy. I think the defining hour came when the legendary Jack Lemmon walked into our dark Hollywood studio on a cold and rainy day without a manager, agent, or bodyguard in tow. Without pomp or circumstance, he politely asked what I would like him to do. Our stylist, Deborah (who was the perfect replacement for a previous stylist who spent too much time lunching at the Armani snack bar), almost fainted from nervousness around Mr. Lemmon. But as one minute of that day dissolved into the next, everyone let go of their anxiety. As rain dripped through a leak in the ceiling of the silent studio, he shared stories of his travels to Africa in pursuit of creating his own photographs. Then he asked if we could switch places so he could do a portrait of me. All I remember was trying to stop shaking as the shutter clicked. This was About Glamour. LEN PRINCE

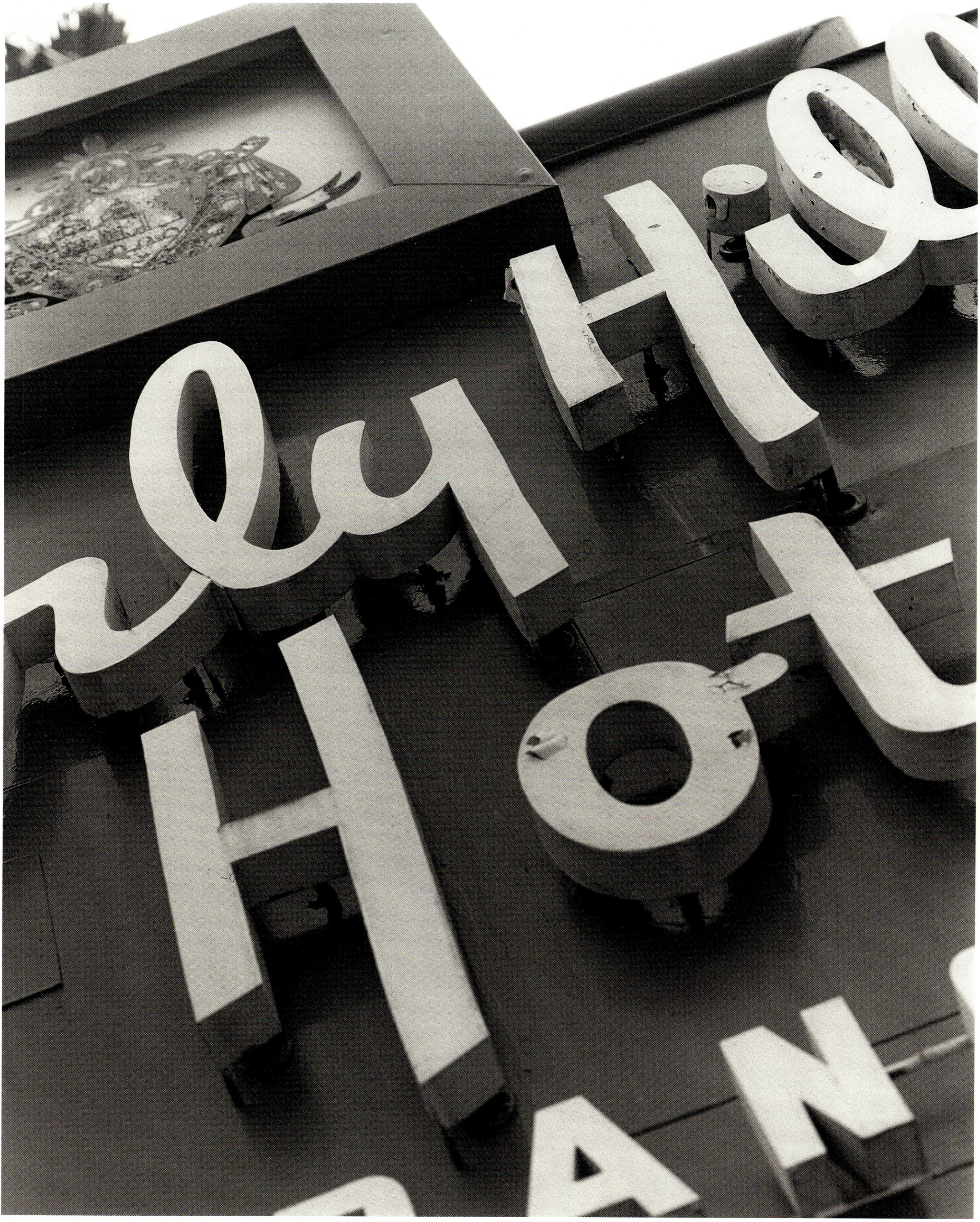

DEDICATION: Westin Hill will always remain my mentor and an uncompromised individual dedicated to living a life of great integrity. I'm always reminded of his contribution and partnership to my ongoing obsessions to create new imagery. If I'm daydreaming, he is there to ring the siren. "Not good enough, try something else" . . . "Move on" . . . "Don't listen to everyone else" . . . "Change the hair" (after someone has worked for two hours) . . . "Who cares!" . . . "It's your name, your picture" . . . "Show more detail, do more!"

West's patience with me has come to bitter ends at time, but through the rubble we always salvage the pearl of wisdom of what's really important about this business and, more important, the journey of a life. West has stood by my side and believed in me when no one else could be found, and no amount of money or fame could ever compete with the value in that hard-won gain. Thank you, West. With love, Len

ACKNOWLEDGMENTS: I wish to thank the following people for the support and dedication they lent to this project: Patti Kramer of Profile and Bruce Kramer of 5th & Sunset Productions, Los Angeles, for their generous donation of facilities and talent; Joe J. Simon for incredible hair and makeup; Peter Davenport, my great friend and photographic subject, who helped expedite the completion of this project; Kelly Bush of Kelly Bush Publicity for her loyalty and outstanding group of talent; Deborah Stambul, a great team player and stylist; a very special thanks to my retoucher, David Joseph, a man with a golden hand and a heart to match; Kelly Klein and Calvin Klein, for their lust for glamour and love of photography; Westin Hill, set design; Patrik Rytikangas for his absolute best as my assistant; Becky Langley and Peter Spirer, whose loyalty never swayed; my friend Robert Sherman for his glamorous makeup artistry; Didier Malige, a truly elegant man, for his work with Kelly Klein; all of the publicists and managers who recognized a special opportunity; lights by Sammy's Camera, Los Angeles; Dusty of Company Collections; Thanks for the Memories; a very special thanks to David Fahey of Fahey/Klein Gallery, Los Angeles; Peter Fetterman Gallery, Santa Monica; Jane Jackson, Atlanta; Staley-Wise Gallery, New York; William Knight Zedwadski; Molly at Giorgio Armani; Randy Smith; Astor Morgan; Barbara Bersell; Lloyd Boston; Stefan Campbell; Edward Wilkerson; my editor, Anne Yarowsky; my gratitude to the Pediatric AIDS Foundation, a very special charity; and last, the Chateau Marmont, my home away from home. L.P.

In memory of Rose and J.J.

A NOTE ON THE TYPE

The text of this book was set in Venetian 301, a refinement of Roman inscriptional capitals designed by Bruce Rogers as a titling for signage in the Metropolitan Museum. Rogers later designed a lowercase based on Jenson's work, turning the titling into a full typeface, the most elegant and Aldine of the Jenson derivatives.

SIMON & SCHUSTER EDITIONS
Rockefeller Center
1230 Avenue of the Americas
New York, NY 10020

Printed and bound in Italy by A. Mondadori Editore
1 3 5 7 9 10 8 6 4 2
Library of Congress Cataloging-in-Publication Data is available.
ISBN 0-684-83623-8

Designed by Sam Shahid

The author intends to donate all royalties due him following publication of the book to the Pediatric AIDS Foundation.

FRONT JACKET:

DEBI MAZAR, NEW YORK CITY, 1993

FRONT MATTER PHOTOGRAPHS:

LEN PRINCE, PHOTOGRAPHED BY LEN PRINCE AND PATRIK RYTIKANGAS, NEW YORK CITY, 1997

DREW BARRYMORE CLOSE-UP, NEW YORK CITY, 1994

INTRODUCTION PHOTOGRAPHS:

STAR MAPS, BEVERLY HILLS, 1994

DOMINICK DUNNE, NEW YORK CITY, 1996

AFTERWORD PHOTOGRAPH:

LEN PRINCE, PHOTOGRAPHED BY WILLIAM CLAXTON, HOLLYWOOD, 1996

BACK MATTER PHOTOGRAPH:

BEVERLY HILLS HOTEL SIGN, SUNSET BOULEVARD, BEVERLY HILLS, 1994

BACK JACKET:

KELLY KLEIN, BEVERLY HILLS, 1994